Praise for *The Happiness Choice*

"As our world seems to move faster, and becomes more impatient and surely complicated, Marilyn Tam offers a soothing, healing perspective on how we can deal with our lives. This thoughtful book to me is all about learning to view the present in a straightforward manner that empowers and energizes our dreams and talents. Healthy, heartfelt wisdom is to be found here."

—Andrew Davis,
Academy Award–nominated film director

"Marilyn Tam offers straightforward, usable advice on how to achieve balance in your life. Happiness in life is a choice, and it is within reach. Marilyn's unique background, her experiences, and her success have given her valuable insights into what it takes to achieve happiness in life. The resources she shares in this book will help you to focus on your life's purpose, prioritize what is truly important, be healthy, and achieve dynamic balance and happiness."

—W. Kenneth Yancey Jr.,
CEO, SCORE Association, resource partner
to the U.S. Small Business Administration

"Your book hit me at the heart. This book is meant for me. This is going to be my textbook to find my life purpose for the rest of my life. It's not too late even at 65 years old. I can rebuild my relationship with my family and I can find my life purpose. A more wonderful life is waiting for me."

—Shoji Tatsuno, Senior Vice President,
Marubeni America Corporation, retired

"Marilyn Tam has done a tremendous service by encouraging us to take a close look at five decisions that illuminate the path of 'relative importance' of our life's robust achievements and propel us to higher levels of meaningful impact and value to the world. This is a must read about the process of 'editing' life as a choice and function to achieving balance."

—Jovita Carranza,
former Vice President for Air Operations,
UPS, and Deputy Administrator,
U.S. Small Business Administration

"Marilyn Tam knows that happiness is a door you open from within. Treasure *The Happiness Choice* and let Marilyn help you find your key and open that door."

—Mark Albion, Faculty Founder of Net Impact,
co-founder of More Than Money Careers,
***New York Times* best-selling author**

"The themes that Marilyn writes about so poignantly are very close to my heart. Having worked through my own personal tragedies to succeed in work and life, I can attest to the power of this life-changing book. Not only does Marilyn share her story, but she gives you a road map you can follow to create the life you really want."

—Libby Gill,
Executive Coach and author of
You Unstuck **and** *Traveling Hopefully*

"What is happiness? There are too many ideas, for various reasons and for different people. No straightforward how-to book can be achieved. But from time to time, new lights are to be gleaned, with insightful suggestions to be considered. Marilyn Tam's new book combines multiple dimensions of these possibilities. May happiness embrace you along the Way, all the Way."

—**Chungliang Al Huang, President-Director,**
Living Tao Foundation–Lan Ting Institute;
author, *Embrace Tiger, Return to Mountain:*
The Essence of Tai Ji; **co-author with Alan Watts,**
Tao: The Watercourse Way; **with Jerry Lynch,**
Thinking Body, Dancing Mind

the HAPPiNESS CHOiCE

HAPPINESS
CHOICE

The 5 Decisions that will take you from where you are to where you want to be

Marilyn Tam

WILEY

John Wiley & Sons, Inc.

Cover design: Paul McCartney

Published by John Wiley & Sons, Inc., Hoboken, New Jersey
Published simultaneously in Canada

For general information about our other products and services, please contact our Customer Care Department within the United States at (800) 762-2974, outside the United States at (317) 572-3993 or fax (317) 572-4002.

Wiley publishes in a variety of print and electronic formats and by print-on-demand. Some material included with standard print versions of this book may not be included in e-books or in print-on-demand. If this book refers to media such as a CD or DVD that is not included in the version you purchased, you may download this material at http://booksupport.wiley.com. For more information about Wiley products, visit www.wiley.com.

Library of Congress Cataloging-in-Publication Data:
Tam, Marilyn.
The happiness choice: the 5 decisions that will take you from where you are to where you want to be / Marilyn Tam.
    p. cm.
Includes index.
ISBN 978-1-118-49316-8 (cloth); 978-1-118-52695-8 (ebk);
ISBN 978-1-118-52670-5 (ebk); ISBN 978-1-118-52660-6 (ebk)
1. Happiness. 2. Self-realization. 3. Conduct of life. I. Title.
BF575.H27T36 2013
158.1–dc23
                                                           2012041498

Printed in the United States of America.

10 9 8 7 6 5 4 3 2 1

CONTENTS

FOREWORD
LOOKING FOR HAPPINESS IN ALL THE RIGHT PLACES

> What we need for our happiness is often close at hand, if we knew but how to seek for it.
>
> *—Nathaniel Hawthorne,*
> *American Note-Books, August 22, 1837*

When I was in high school, seeking happiness through my studies, and, well, okay—through the tortured pursuit of love—I read a short story by Nathaniel Hawthorne that has stuck with me for half a century. It is titled *The Birthmark*.

The story is an allegory about looking for happiness in all the wrong places. Alymer, a great scientist, loves his magnificently beautiful wife Georgina passionately. But she has a small flaw, a scarlet birthmark on her cheek in the shape of a tiny hand. Obsessed with the imperfection, Alymer devotes himself to removing it. After considerable labor he invents a potion, which his dutiful wife swallows to very ill effect.

Hawthorne describes her death in an unforgettable way: "The fatal hand had grappled with the mystery of life, and was the bond by which an angelic spirit kept itself in union with a mortal frame. As the last crimson tint of the birthmark—that sole token of human imperfection—faded from her cheek, the parting breath of the now perfect woman passed into the atmosphere, and her soul, lingering a moment near her husband, took its heavenward flight."

Being a young romantic when I read the story, Georgina's swooning form left an indelible impression on my psyche. It symbolized the foolishness of thinking that if only we were perfect, or someone else were perfect, or life was fair then we would be happy. "I'll be happy when . . ." is the illusion that stands between us and the wholehearted act of engaging fully with life, moment by moment, here and now. It is that deep engagement—whether through love, work, service, or simply wandering through the meadows and feeling the warmth of the sun that creates the variety of emotional states that we call happiness.

What do we actually mean by happiness? The deep contentment and love that a mother experiences when nursing her baby? The transcendent feeling of finding our beloved? The sense of belonging and security afforded by strong family ties? The excitement of a child, counting down the days to Christmas or a birthday? The accomplishment that comes from completing a meaningful task? The sense of homecoming when faith reveals our place in the universe? The excitement of sex or even of eating a chocolate cupcake?

University of Pennsylvania professor of psychology, Dr. Martin E. P. Seligman, is the founder of the field called Positive Psychology. He has written widely about happiness and coined the acronym PERMA as a summary of decades of research into what creates well-being and human flourishing.[1] Seligman's main point is that you can't remove unhappiness and expect well-being. You get emptiness instead. The trick to finding happiness is to look for it in all the right places—the five dimensions of well-being.

---

[1] Martin E. P. Seligman, *Flourish: A Visionary New Understanding of Happiness and Well-being*, reprint ed. (New York: Free Press, 2012).

1. Pleasure that induces positive emotions (think massage, great food, creature comforts, sex, doing good for others).

2. Engagement (creating a sense of flow, as when you lose track of time pursuing an activity that is both fun and challenging).

3. Relationships (love and connection may be the number one happiness maker for us social animals).

4. Meaning (that wonderful spiritual sense of belonging to a larger whole).

5. Accomplishments (reaching your goals).

A neglected dimension in Seligman's model is the body. Exercise, nutrition, and the cultivation of inner balance through yoga or tai chi. Fortunately, this dimension is an important part of the book that you're now holding in your hands.

My friend and colleague, Marilyn Tam, is a truly happy person—and by that I don't mean a perfect person or one who has everything. Marilyn is a resilient person who is relentlessly creative and invested in living a meaningful life for the benefit of others. As a business executive, humanitarian, and avid student of life, she has identified the core dimensions of well-being and happiness through studying people who are exemplars of what it is to have a well-balanced life (a dynamic concept, believe me!) that fosters well-being in the core areas of relationship, finance, spirituality, life purpose, and care of the body.

For me, the stories of people's lives are the most instructive and inspiring way to learn. While I know several of the people who Marilyn interviewed personally, it was a pleasure (and therefore very happiness making!) to read more of their stories. When Marilyn approached me with the idea for this book I was thrilled to collaborate by suggesting people to interview. Our many talks about this book—and the healthy smoothies that Marilyn whipped up during a visit she made to our home—were the essence of PERMA. I made a choice for happiness by helping Marilyn realize her vision for this book. Now you've made a choice for happiness by reading it.

—**Joan Borysenko, PhD**

PREFACE

O
ne early morning, during her annual visit to Hong Kong, my mother had a massive stroke alone in her bed. She laid there, eyes wide with terror, unable to move, gurgling and rasping for help until her friend in the next room found her. My mother, who once arrived at my future place of employment—the corporate headquarters of Reebok International Inc.—unannounced, demanding to see the CEO and chairman and her daughter's new office. Unsurprising but painfully embarrassing to me when I found out later, the CEO, my boss-to-be, actually took a break from the company's corporate board meeting to show my mother around the building. This woman, who was so used to getting whatever she wanted, is now totally without voice or physical movement and at the mercy of her caregivers.

As I sat next to her, massaging her hands and singing to her, I reflected on life. Are you living the life of your dreams? What if you woke up one day immobilized and gasping? Would you be at peace or would you wish that you had chosen to live your life differently?

In 2011, as I was writing my small book, *Living the Life of Your Dreams*, a mini handbook and an introduction to this book, I received a wonderful gift. My friend, colleague, and inspiration, Joan Borysenko, PhD, sent me her new book, *Fried: Why You Burn Out and How to Revive*. I read it with increasing wonder— we were converging on the same place—the reasons for unhappiness: poor emotional, physical, and financial health and how to establish a new dynamic balance of joy, vitality, love, and success.

I dashed off my manuscript to Joan immediately and proposed that we jointly write the next book—*The Happiness Choice*. Joan had a prior book commitment, which prevented her from co-authoring this book, but she enthusiastically and generously offered to share and guide me every step of the way. This book is the result of our collaboration, along with the wisdom and insight of many other experts who will reveal how you can juggle the many demands on your time and energy in pursuit of your own personal fulfillment. It's possible, and in fact necessary, to live a life of dynamic balance. It's your happiness choice.

> Success is not the key to happiness. Happiness is the key to success. If you love what you are doing, you will be successful.
>
> —*Albert Schweitzer (1875–1965)*

INTRODUCTION

Y ou wake before the alarm, turn over, and then it hits you—you are already behind on what you have to do today. Out of bed you rush to get ready, grab something to eat, gulp down some coffee and *zoom* your nerves are already vibrating at hyper speed. At the end of the long and exhausting day, you fall into bed bone-tired and weary, feeling that you didn't accomplish many of the things you had to do, much less the ones you wanted to do. Sigh, is this the life I was born to live, you wonder.

No! You have a choice; you can live the life that you've dreamed of living. You can choose happiness.

"Hah," you say, "What is that? I would settle for having a life!" Yes, I understand, I have been there. I know the edgy, nagging feeling that gnaws at your insides and buzzes in your brain as you juggle more demands than humanly possible. There *is* another way and I am delighted to share that with you. Come with us on this journey to discover and fulfill your birthright—to live the life that you've always wanted.

Joan and I did not come from privilege. Our early years were hard, and we both had a good number of devastating challenges in our later years, too. However, those are the very things that we give thanks for—our "training" gave us the understanding, insights, and skills to achieve lives that surpass our wildest dreams.

I am the second daughter in a traditional Chinese family, and my birth was followed quickly by the birth of three younger brothers. To say that I was unwanted would be an understatement—my mother left me in the hospital and had to be called to pick me up. My inauspicious entry into the world foretold years of physical and mental mistreatment. Rising from an abusive childhood and leaving my home in Hong Kong as a teen for university in the United States alone, to becoming a global business leader and humanitarian, I've found the secrets to achieving a better life than I'd ever dreamed was possible—and you can, too.

Now I live in Santa Barbara, California, walking distance to the ocean and the mountains, sharing a sunny, spacious, and cozy home with the love of my life. I have retired from the corporate executive world to run my global speaking and consulting business, pursue my writing, and manage the non-profit charitable foundation I co-founded.

As I look out the window of my home office, I see trees laden with ripening oranges, lemons, and avocados in my organic garden, while the roses in the flowerbeds vie with them for abundance and glory. On the other side, the pool is glistening in the sunlight, white and yellow plumeria flowers are wafting their sweet scent, the palm fronds and bamboo leaves are fluttering gently while the hummingbirds hover over the geraniums, lilies and irises are blooming in front of the little meditation house. Ah, indeed, I am so thankful for my life.

Joan also has gone through devastating hardships of emotional and financial deceit but she, too, is finally living the life of her dreams. Joan has learned and grown from many tough life lessons.

Now she is living with her beloved and loving husband, Gordie, in a home of their design on a pristine Colorado mountaintop. They work together on far-reaching transformative and healing projects that fulfill both their professional and personal goals. They take time to walk the labyrinth that they built on the wild flower-covered knoll that they live on and to hike with their dogs among the pine trees and woodlands that is their backyard. Their children and grandchildren come regularly to visit and share in the love and beauty that they have created. Joan and Gordie have woven their work, personal time, and play time into a fulfilling, productive, and nurturing life fabric that they share in joy.

It is from this place of gratitude that this book is written for you, so that you, too, can have the life you want and deserve: a happy, balanced, and healthy life. For more information, visit www.MarilynTam.com.

> Remember, happiness doesn't depend upon who you are or what you have; it depends solely upon what you think.
> —*Dale Carnegie*

1

THIS IS NOT THE
LIFE I THOUGHT
I WAS LIVING

Born into a very traditional Chinese family in Hong Kong, I was the second daughter of parents who were desperate for a son. Then my mother gave birth to three boys and cemented my position at the bottom of the totem pole. With three younger brothers I grew up an unwanted, neglected, and abused child in a culture where dirt was more valuable than a useless second daughter.

My one blessing was the name given to me by my grandfather. A very unusual honor for a Chinese girl, he named me Hay Lit after two respected Chinese emperors. This proud name empowered me to grow up believing that someone in my family cared about my future and inspired me to think that one day I could do something important with my life.

I knew there were other children who were much worse off than me. One of my schoolmates and her family of five lived in a single room where they shared a kitchen and bath with two other families. With both parents working, my friend still didn't have proper clothing or enough food to eat. It didn't seem fair that she had to live this way. At the age of 11, I knew that making a positive difference and helping people in need was my true destiny.

As a teenager, I came to the United States alone for a college education. I was driven to making positive change in the world. Working my way through school, I completed my undergraduate studies and earned a master's degree. From the bottom of the totem pole, I climbed to the top of the corporate ladder in high-level executive positions at well-known international companies (vice president at Nike Inc., president of Reebok Apparel & Retail Group, CEO at Aveda Corp.). From there I became an entrepreneur, author (*How to Use What You've Got to Get What You Want* is now in several languages, and *Living the Life of Your Dreams* won the Global eBook of the Year 2011 award in the Inspirational/Visionary category), and co-founded a nonprofit organization (Us Foundation) dedicated to promoting the highest common good for humanity and the planet. I even received an honorary doctorate from Old Dominion University in Virginia for the body of work I've done over the years. Wow, if only I knew all this would happen when I was young, alone, and scared.

Along the way, I never forgot my life's purpose: to make a positive difference. As an executive in the apparel industry, one of my proudest accomplishments was helping to create positive change in labor standards for workers in developing countries.

Some years ago, in addition to running my foundation, I was writing, speaking, and consulting with global companies and governmental organizations on leadership, diversity, life balance, and other business issues, and through my health and wellness center, teaching clients around the world how to enjoy a balanced and healthy lifestyle.

Then one day, my sister, who lives in Vancouver, B.C., called and said that she wanted to come to California and spend Christmas with me. "I'm sorry," I heard myself say to my sister who I dearly love and hadn't seen for over two years, "but I'm just too tired to even think about the holidays. In fact, I'm going to cancel Christmas entirely this year."

Listening to myself, I thought, "What am I saying? This is just ridiculous! This is crazy!" I suddenly realized that in giving so much to help other people, I had completely forgotten about taking care of my personal needs. The truth hit me like a ton of bricks. I was shocked and embarrassed. My own labor standards were completely out of balance! The second daughter, Hay Lit, had been putting *herself* at the bottom of the totem pole.

My sister was speechless at first, but then she understood that I was just so burned out. I realized then that my priorities were all mixed up. Because I had been giving everything I had to other people and to so many worthy causes, at the end of the year I had nothing left for me—or my own sister!

Travelling around the world, I had been teaching business, nonprofit and government leaders to honor their physical and emotional health, spend time with family and friends, and pursue their intellectual interests and spiritual calling. But I had not made time to do many of these things myself. Could pushing oneself beyond her limits into a state of total exhaustion be an example of low self-worth, self-neglect, or even self-abuse?

Reflecting upon how the role of women in the United States has changed, I realized that today we are expected to wear many different hats—daughter, friend, career woman, wife, mother, and community leader. Juggling all these things, we struggle to stay in shape, look beautiful, have a spiritual core, and become self-actualized—expectations that we, as well as society, have placed upon us. Every now and then, we have to stop ourselves and ask, "Am I taking care of the most important person in the world?" Yes, that's you.

While keeping all the traditional roles, women of our generation have taken on many additional responsibilities. Multitasking comes naturally to the female gender leading us to believe that we can do everything, all the time, and all at once. But this is impossible, and sometimes in order to achieve what's critical and to remain sane, we just have to say no.

Whenever you feel overwhelmed, stop, take a deep breath, and then take another one, and then ask, "What would happen if I didn't do this task at this very moment? What is really most important? What is the truth here for me?" Pull yourself back enough to get distance and perspective. Listen to the voice of your inner wisdom. The answer will come.

In order to stay true to my life's purpose, I have learned to put my own needs high on the list of priorities and practice what I preach. Only by striving to make certain that my life is sustained in a balanced way can I make the positive difference that is my destiny.

After all, how can I help to heal the world if I can't take care of me? And you? Are you neglecting yourself to take care of others? Is that really working for you and your loved ones? When you are giving from *lack*—it's unsustainable and will eventually not only drain you but destroy the very relationships and structures you are working so hard to build.

Stop, take a deep breath, and repeat the above instructions as needed. Remember that you are part of the whole—if you neglect or abuse yourself and become a hole—instead of a valuable part of the whole—the whole will also have a hole.

Yes, we know the bills have to be paid and the work assignment and laundry done—somehow all *will* get done. Believe us, it will. Continue to read with us, please; this book will show you the way.

> I have come to the frightening conclusion that I am the decisive element.
> It is my personal approach that creates the climate.
> It is my daily mood that makes the weather.
> I possess tremendous power to make life miserable or joyous.
> I can be a tool of torture or an instrument of inspiration.
> I can humiliate or humor, hurt or heal.
> In all situations, it is my response that decides whether a crisis is escalated or de-escalated, and a person is humanized or de-humanized.
> If we treat people as they are, we make them worse.
> If we treat people as they ought to be, we help them become what they are capable of becoming.
> —*Johann Wolfgang von Goethe, 1749–1832*

2

UPTURN,
DOWNTURN,
YOUR TURN

For a long time it had seemed to me that life was about to begin—real life. But there was always some obstacle in the way. Something to be got through first, some unfinished business, time still to be served, a debt to be paid. Then life would begin. At last it dawned on me that these obstacles were my life.

—*Fr. Alfred D'Souza*

D o you often say: "I'll do that when—and the "when" is all about someone or something else? I'll do it when work is less busy, when my parent/child/spouse/partner/friend demands less of me, or when there is more time or money so that I feel okay about allocating some for my own needs. The cause may be very noble; you are dedicated to your passion, to your family, to your job—whatever it may be. The running theme is that someone or something else takes precedence over your personal needs. Your work, family, friends, community, and/or your humanitarian work have priority in your life over you. It/they are demanding more than you have to give and it seems that even that is still not enough.

Many people die with their music still in them. Why is this so? Too often it is because they are always getting ready to live. Before they know it, time runs out.

—*Oliver Wendell Holmes*

We read regularly about the upturn and downturn in the economy. When is it your turn? Your turn is *now*. Time to take care of you. Wait, you say, what I am doing now is very important, if I don't do it, things will fall apart! I say if you continue this way, *you* will fall apart. Or maybe you already feel like you are crumbling inside and that is why you are reading— welcome, you have come to the right place.

When I am anxious it is because I am living in the future.

When I am depressed it is because I am living in the past.
                                        —*Author unknown*

Joan Borysenko, PhD, in her book, *Fried: Why You Burn Out and How to Revive*,[1] devotes much discussion to this very topic. You can only perform optimally and take care of others when you are feeling properly nourished, physically, mentally, emotionally, and spiritually. When we are working "tirelessly" and giving with little consideration of our own needs, we burn out. Joan speaks about the Yerkes-Dodson law, which outlines the relationship between stress and burnout. The inverse U curve of stress versus productivity, with productivity on the y-axis (vertical line) of the graph and stress on the x-axis (horizontal line) shows that the initial positive correlation between stress and productivity becomes an increasing hindrance to further productivity and growth after a point. You have to work a lot harder and still get less work of a poorer quality done when that threshold of stress has been exceeded—and eventually burnout occurs and life becomes mundane and meaningless, to say the least.

Joan cites the work of psychologist Herbert Freudenberger and how he defines burnout: "the extinction of motivation or incentive, especially where one's devotion to a cause or relationship fails to produce the desired results." Does any of this sound familiar? I know it does to me, I've experienced it more than once, and that is why it is my passion to share with you what I have learned in my journey back to a dynamically balanced, rich, and joyous life.

---

[1] Joan Borysenko, *Fried: Why You Burn Out and How to Revive* (Carlsbad, CA: Hay House, 2011).

Many women are living on the edge of their capacity, especially women with children. *Working Mother* magazine did a survey in 2010 that showed that many working mothers, who appear to be in total control, are actually under severe stress. Forty percent of the respondents said they drink heavily to cope with stress, and 57 percent reported that they have misused prescription drugs. And both of these figures look set to rise, says Suzann Riss, *Working Mother*'s editor-in-chief.

And it is not just working mothers but all women who are feeling stressed and relatively less happy and fulfilled than in previous years. There are many large-scale studies on happiness levels among men and women nationally and internationally, and the sad fact is that women all over the world report experiencing less joy and more burdens.

The United States General Social Survey has conducted an annual happiness survey since 1972 among a representative sample of men and women (about 50,000 people so far) of all ages, education levels, income levels, and marital status, asking: "How happy are you, on a scale of 1 to 3, with 3 being very happy, and 1 being not too happy?"

One of the most notable results is that women's overall level of happiness has decreased compared to what it was 40 years ago—and to men. And the drop occurs regardless of their financial position, marital status, children, age, or race. The lone exception is that African American women report being a little happier now than when the survey launched in 1972, but they are still less happy than African American men.

Other countries show the same trend. The British Household Panel Study, Eurobarometer Analysis (15 countries), and the International Social Survey Program (35 developed nations) both point toward this same concerning fact. Women are feeling more and unhappy in the past few decades and it is a global phenomenon.[2]

There are many numbers crunchers and social scientists who have more diligently combed through the many studies and statistics than I will ever do. The consensus from all their work is inconclusive as to why women aren't happier—it appears that economically, careerwise, socially, financially, and relationshipwise women have made significant headway since the studies first started tracking happiness. How is it possible that women are falling behind in happiness absolutely and relatively?

May I postulate an answer? That even though statistically all major factors in a woman's life seem to have improved, the recent (past 30-plus years) expectations of a woman's role have been bolted on to the old stereotypes of a woman's traditional role. We women are now expected to perform dual stereotypical roles—the traditional daughter, wife, mother, homemaker, and community service volunteer is now also supposed to be a career woman, well-versed in economic, political, and social affairs, and she must exercise, eat right, look good, have a loving relationship with a suitable (attractive and wealthy) mate, a meaningful spiritual life, and make it all look easy in the process! We have bought the image society has created for us, and most women struggle valiantly and vainly in our own ways to fulfill it. No wonder women are unhappy; it is an impossible list of accomplishments for anyone to achieve without burning herself up in trying.

Men have it a bit easier, but just a little: they are less tied to the traditional men's roles now, and they are allowed to show

---

[2] For more information, see Marcus Buckingham's book, *Find Your Strongest Life*, (Nashville, TN: Thomas Nelson, 2009).

their feelings more but they are now also expected to be more rounded in their pursuits—help out more around the house, be more involved as fathers, and yes, work on their own physical, emotional, and spiritual sides, too. For some men this is a daunting list. Welcome to the new world where the media has raised the expectations of what each person is supposed to achieve to the level only possible in the fantasyland of commercials, movies, TV, and the Internet.

> Nobody can go back and start a new beginning, but anyone
> can start today and make a new ending.
> —*Maria Robinson*

Okay, how do you start to get out of dangerous stress and into some semblance of dynamic life balance? First, by acknowledging that there are just too many things on your plate. Then review your options and allocate attention and resources according to how you value each area of your life. I've often been asked when I give talks around the world, "Can you have it all?" To many in the audiences, it seems that I have it all and I have to laugh and say:

> Yes, you can have it all, but not usually all at the same time.

It is all about priorities. In the next chapter we will discuss how to find your life mission. When you know your purpose for being alive, it is easy to judge the relative importance of every demand on your emotional, physical, financial, and spiritual energies.

> Every choice before you represents the universe inviting you
> to remember who you are and what you want.
> —*Alan Cohen*

Judi Weisbart's company is called A Busy Woman Consulting.[3] The old saying, "when you want something done, you ask a busy person" was the inspiration for her company's name. Yet Judi lives a life of dynamic balance—she balances consulting, event planning, and fund-raising for nonprofits in her business, with her sculpting, painting, and pottery for gallery shows and sales, her volunteer work on women's and peace issues globally, time with her husband and four now-grown children and, oh, her 92-year-old mother lives with them, too. And yes, she regularly takes time out to go swimming at her club's Olympic-sized pool and to meditate so that she can maintain her physical and mental health.

Judi says that it all works because she believes in connection and community. "We are in relationship and community with other people, and it is not our job to do everything. If you feel overwhelmed, ask for help and edit what you think you have to do. Eliminate the things that are of low priority. Everyone is in a dance, you don't have to lead all the time—you are only exhausted when you are doing it all without asking for help." It is your turn now to ask for help.

By age 25 Judi was a stepmother to three teenagers with a newborn child and a husband. To manage the demands on her time, she asked for help: her stepchildren set the table, washed dishes, and handled other chores, and her husband did his share of household tasks. Wonderfully, everyone gained when they worked together as a family. The children and her husband felt more involved and responsible, and it fostered increased feelings of being a family unit. Judi gave an example of what she meant by reframing the way we look at life—the father is not baby-sitting the child when the mother has to do something else, he is taking care of and connecting with his child. It is a more realistic

---

[3] www.abusywoman.com, www.judiweisbart.com.

way of looking at the situation. When we look at the circumstances and see them factually, it relieves the misplaced guilt
that people, especially women, feel when they are not doing
everything by themselves.

Women are trained and culturally conditioned to do it all—
women have to remember that they are not the only responsible
person in the relationship. This also happens to business leaders
of both genders; oftentimes they are afraid to ask for help on
what they consider their job—to make decisions. When the
person in charge brings together others to strategize on goals
and action plans, the implementation is easily embraced and
executed because the people closer to the endeavor are more
deeply involved and the results are also better. Ask the other
people involved to actively participate; you will be amazed how
well it works after the initial surprise. Look inside, are you doing
too much out of ego (the need to have control) or out of what
you were taught to do—instead of realizing that you are in a
community/group/company and each person has to fully participate for optimal functioning? Upturn, downturn, it is always
your turn to take care of yourself before you can truly handle any
other task.

> A rock pile ceases to be a rock pile the moment a single
> person contemplates it, bearing within the image of a
> cathedral.
>
> —*Antoine de Saint-Exupéry*

3

LIFE PURPOSE— YOURS

These are the two most important days in your life:

1. The day you were born
2. The day you found out why you were born

—A humanitarian upon receiving an award for his work

Do you remember your dreams from when you were a child? You wanted to be some type of hero—someone who was inspiring for you—a cartoon character, a TV personality, a figure from a storybook, an inspiring family member, or some mystical creature that could magically transform your surroundings to the happy, fun place you hoped it would be. What happened to that dream?

Chances are it was squashed by other people's expectations of you. "What are you going to be when you grow up?" people would ask. The acceptable answer usually was what they wanted to hear rather than what you felt was your life's calling. You were supposed to be responsible, aiming for something that other people thought was proper and right for you. Your own hopes, dreams, and talents were almost an afterthought to them in many ways. They were seeing you through the lens of their own conditioning. Oftentimes, what they wanted you to take on was what they did or wished they had done; it had much more to do with their own hopes and fears than yours.

Then there is the media—glamorizing certain roles: movie and TV stars; athletes; rock stars; major business moguls; and the rich, indulged children of people with enormous wealth; and other unrealistic role models. These celebrities seemed to live charmed lives with little accountability and with nothing as mundane as bills to pay, dishes and laundry to do. Those subliminal messages crept into your mind, burrowed in deep, and emerged whenever you had a setback in your life; they made you feel inadequate, wanting, and unhappy.

Bombarded by the relentless conditioning of what you are supposed to be, you packed your own dreams away, so hidden that you may have forgotten that you ever had them. You internalized the message that society gave you: that you have to be rich, famous, multitalented, good-looking, and in excellent physical shape to be happy. Of course you also have to be accomplished in a profession, keep a beautiful home, have well-behaved and smart children, be self actualized, spiritual, do community service, and give back to the world. Oh, and you need to have the right—that is, rich, glamorous, and good-looking—partner on your arm to complete the picture. No wonder you may be confused as to your life's mission!

> I don't think I have ever worked in my life, because work to
> me means that you are really doing something you don't like.
> —*John Kluge, multibillionaire founder of Metromedia*

Maybe you are one of the fortunate few who found their life's purpose early and have stayed the course all your life. I am blessed to say that I am one of them. How do you find your reason for being? In my case it was through the realization that the world is a lot bigger when I am open to seeing it from other people's perspectives.

I was shunted off to live with my aunt and uncle when I was seven in the hope that they would adopt me. They had no children after many failed attempts, and my parents had two daughters and three sons already. As the second daughter I was dispensable, and, in fact, as my mother frequently reminded me, I was worthless.

Staying with my aunt and uncle in the little fishing village where they lived exposed me to people of meager means who were nevertheless happy and productive. They liked the freedom of their lifestyle of being outdoors and in nature doing something they loved. My friends were the poor fishermen children and the child factory piecework workers with whom I worked. We assembled plastic flowers and embroidered needlepoint handbags at home or at special gathering places on the streets for pennies. Yet, I was comfortable. No one told me I was useless.

Then life changed again. My aunt gave birth to their first child, a son. I was sent back to live with my parents again. This gave me an even sharper understanding of what it means to be unwanted.

School uniforms are great equalizers; we have no idea of the relative wealth of each other. Without distinguishing clothes we lose a tool that is often used to judge other people. Rebecca, one of my classmates, turned out to be from a family of paltry financial means. With two working parents, my friend and her family lived in one room and shared a kitchen and bathroom with two other families. Often they didn't have enough to eat.

I was filled with outrage when I found this out. It didn't seem fair or reasonable that in spite of all their best efforts a family couldn't maintain the basics of life. I realized that no matter how bad my life might seem to me, there were people who had it worse, much worse. No, not as some remote concept from TV, magazines, or books (this was before the Internet, after all), but a real life person whom I knew was facing true hardship.

I vowed that I would grow up to help others attain what we all want—freedom from basic wants and happiness. My life mission was set; I was going to save the world. I was 11 years old.

It sometimes takes a defining event like my discovery of Rebecca's home situation to ignite the inner passion of what drives us. Other times, your life passion may be so hidden that you are not consciously aware of it yet. But everyone has one. Finding out what yours is will propel you to another level of existence, one in which you are motivated to do what you are destined to do.

> Your time is limited, so don't waste it living someone else's life. Don't be trapped by dogma—which is living with the results of other people's thinking. Don't let the noise of others' opinions drown out your own inner voice. And most important, have the courage to follow your heart and intuition. They somehow already know what you truly want to become. Everything else is secondary.
>
> —*Steve Jobs*

Joan Borysenko shared her own journey to finding her life purpose. Now looking back, she realized that she discovered her life purpose in a defining event at age 10, but it then took many years of development for her life mission to fully emerge as it is today. So it may be with you, your mission may have appeared as a shining glimmer at one time. Whether you followed it consciously or subconsciously or were distracted by something else, it is still there deep within you.

When Joan was 10, her parents took her to a horror movie that featured poisonous snakes, headhunters, and ferocious animals in the jungle. She was deeply frightened, and she believed that she and her family could face similar terrors. Being a precocious and sensitive child, Joan developed a belief that the only way her family could be saved was by what psychologists now define as an obsessive-compulsive ritual to keep harm away. She adopted a series of behaviors—hand washing, specific sayings, and other rituals—which she performed repeatedly throughout the day.

Understandably alarmed, Joan's parents took her to a therapist to seek help. Joan's behavior was so consuming that she was held back from attending school and her beloved Jewish girls' camp, which was upcoming. Upon learning that she would be denied many things that gave her joy, Joan prayed fervently for help. In that place of prayer and reflection she found a powerful sense of peace and love, and she realized she could heal herself. She had to stop all her ritualistic behaviors at once, cold turkey. And with the inner peace she received from her deep prayer, she found the strength and wisdom to stop the rituals completely.

After she regained balance, Joan realized that what she experienced was a profound spiritual phenomenon and wondered if other people had similar experiences. She wanted to bring back that sense of enveloping love and peace she felt at that time. It became Joan's life mission to understand and develop that deep sense of stillness, wellness, and love and to share that with others. How does a child go from being normal and well-functioning to obsessive-compulsive and back again? She wanted to find out; she was going to become a psychiatrist when she grew up.

Joan majored in biology and psychology at Bryn Marr and worked at Wyeth Labs researching objective conditioning while she was in school. She was fascinated by the advances in neuroscience and cell biology and entered Harvard Medical School to study for her doctorate in cell biology. Along the way she had many inspiring mentors who guided her and her research in biofeedback and in cell biology on how cells interact with each other, the primary communication system that determines our body's health. Her interest in cell biology and biofeedback led her into cancer research.

Joan flourished in her work, and for a while she was teaching and doing research at both Tufts Medical School and Harvard Medical School. It was a fascinating and energizing time. And then tragedy struck. Joan's beloved father was diagnosed with a virulent form of leukemia and was given large doses of steroids that left him unable to think clearly and caused severe psychosis. During a small window of time when he was taken off the steroids for another operation, he realized his mental condition and committed suicide rather than face the prospect of being put back on the steroids that would render him again incapable of normal cognitive functioning.

Joan was devastated—a cancer biology expert who could not help her own father. She switched from full time research to more working with people and helping them use all the tools of mind, body, and spirit to regain and maintain health. She started sharing the entire body of work she was integrating, from the newest medical science, to the ancient wisdom of yoga, meditation, and prayer. It was a transformative and exciting time for Joan as well as others involved in the field of understanding the role of mind, body, and spirit in health and well-being.

In her relentless zeal and fervor, Joan's overworked world came crashing down, literally. She was severely hurt in a car crash. It was a wake-up call. She could not sustain her research, clinical work with patients, writing leading-edge books[1] on her work, and all the while being a good mother to her teenage sons and maintaining a meaningful relationship with her husband— much less keep up her physical and mental health, too.

It was time for her to truly embody what she learned when she was 10 years old. She was primed and ready to follow her life purpose of developing inner peace, wellness, and love and to share the process with others. Joan resigned from her Harvard post and devoted her time and energy to writing, speaking, and to her personal and family life. It took Joan many years from that 10-year-old's first inner knowing to fully living her mission. And when Joan looks back, she says that each step along the way was blessed with mentors, synchronicities, and lessons that lead her to her following her life mission.

---

[1] Joan Borysenko, *Minding the Body, Mending the Mind* (New York: Bantam Doubleday Dell, 1997).

Joan Borysenko, Ph.D., a pioneer in integrative medicine and a world-renowned expert in the mind (body health connection and the spiritual dimensions of life as an integral part of health and healing. For more photos and information of all the experts in the book, please go to www.MarilynTam.com

And that can also be true for you. You may not be completely clear on your life purpose and what makes you happy. Keep leaning into it. Ask yourself why a particular situation is developing the way it is. What can you learn? Are you moving closer or further away from what you want? Like a sunflower that always grows facing the sun, are you turning toward what gives you energy and life, or are you moving away?

Pursue your passion. We are all born with our own set of unique talents. We were put on this earth to serve a purpose and pursue what it is we are truly passionate about. Identifying, acknowledging, and honoring this purpose is perhaps the most important action successful people take. They take the time to understand what they're here to do—and then pursue that with passion and enthusiasm.

Jack Canfield discovered long ago what he was put on this earth to do: inject passion and determination into every activity he undertook. Jack learned how having purpose can bring an aspect of fun and fulfillment to virtually everything he does.

Jack's mission statement is as follows: "You have to believe it's possible and believe in yourself. Because after you've decided what you want, you have to believe it's possible, and possible for you, not just for other people. Then you need to seek out models, mentors, and coaches."[2]

THE FOUR STAGES IN LIFE

Each person goes through four stages in life. The good news is that you may revert to an earlier stage to learn and grow more regardless of your age. This is encouraging, indeed, because historically we have been conditioned to think that life is strictly chronological: you are born, go through the learning years, enter the producing and generating phase, then embark on the maturity stage, and lastly begin to share from your experience and flow gracefully—or not—into the final season of life. That was the traditional perspective and generally, especially in regards to our physical bodies, it is mostly accurate.

However, with improved understanding and advances in nutrition, exercise, health care, and longevity, our bodies may now be even healthier and more vibrant than when we were chronologically younger. There are definite physical and psychological stages of development in each person's life, and we

---

[2] Jack Canfield, America's number one Success Coach, is founder of the billion-dollar book brand, *Chicken Soup for the Soul*, and a leading authority on Peak Performance and Life Success. www.freesuccessstrategies.com

have opportunities to revisit these phases later in life.[3] Of course we cannot completely dial back our body's time clock as many a woman who has delayed too long in having biological children can tell you, but we now have a better understanding of how to maximize our vitality and augment our well-being.

The same is true for our working lives. We can go from the development stage, to producing, on to reevaluation and wisdom and back to additional learning (development) and generating (production), more analysis (reevaluation) and wisdom. See Figure 3.1. In fact, in today's world, it is more common for people to have multiple jobs and careers than to stay in one career all their lives.[4] And older workers (55–64 years, median tenure: 10.0 years) are currently three times more likely to stay at their jobs than younger ones (25–34 years, median tenure: 3.1 years).

What this may indicate is that more and more people are reassessing and going back to a previous stage in the cycle—a very good thing if you feel unsatisfied and unfulfilled with your career or your life's direction; you can change it more easily than ever before. You can have another chance at choosing what makes you happy.

This is indeed good news because research has shown that people who have a definite life purpose are healthier and have significantly less Alzheimer's disease and mental deterioration than people who do not have a clear reason for living.[5]

---

[3] Abraham Maslow's "Hierarchy of Needs" and Erik Erickson's "Eight Stages of Human Development."

[4] U.S. Bureau of Labor statistics show that in 2010 the median worker held the same job for 4.4 years, a 0.3-year increase from 2008 because of the greater loss of jobs for the less senior workers during the recession. Younger workers also stayed at the same job for a shorter period of time (three times shorter).

[5] Rush University Medical Center, *Archives of General Psychiatry* (May 2012).

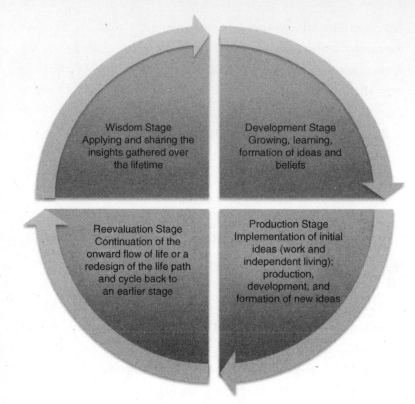

Figure 3.1 The four stages in life

Jack Canfield was in his junior year at Harvard University when a chance encounter prompted him to do a reevaluation of his life purpose. At that point, Jack was studying to be a teacher; his goal was to teach in the inner city. He had a deep desire, borne from his agonizing experiences growing up with an abusive and drunk father, to help other children. During that fateful afternoon at the Newport Folk Festival, Jack serendipitously sat next to Pete Seeger, the famous folk singer and composer. He was heartened by his idol's openness and warmth toward him, an ordinary student and fan. He was deeply affected and understood at a visceral level the power of human connection and music to impact lives. Jack's experience with Pete Seeger and the social issues sung about at the folk festival made a lasting and transformative impression on Jack.

Jack was inspired to reassess how to apply his energies to achieve the positive change in the world that he wanted to make. Back at school, Jack took a course entitled Social Relations 10, which opened his mind to the work of the pioneers in the Human Potential Movement. That pivotal festival encouraged Jack to more clearly define his life mission, and now he is globally known and respected as a leader in the field of human potential and personal transformation. Jack entered the reevaluation process very early in life compared with many people; a good number have not even determined their first career goal by the middle of their undergraduate studies.[6]

His story is an illustration of how, if you are present to what is happening at the moment, you can learn so much more and conceivably even change your life. For the great number of people who may not yet know their life purpose, there is hope. For each person who found his or her life mission early in life, there are many more who discover it much later.

Chellie Campbell, creator of the popular Financial Stress Reduction Workshops,[7] is one who discovered her life purpose later in life. She realized it at age 42. Then she published her first book at 54, and her second book at 58. Now, at 64 years old, she's more energized and motivated than ever before. Her advice for people who don't know their life mission yet is to relax, move toward what calls to you most. Don't struggle— your best guess will do for now. Follow what you feel is your purpose, and as you follow that you will find out more.

---

[6] Jack Canfield and William Gladstone, *The Golden Motorcycle Gang* (Carlsbad, CA: Hay House, 2011).

[7] Chellie Campbell, www.Chellie.com

Chellie started out as a musical comedy actress, before that she was fascinated by archaeology and wanted to be the next Howard Carter and the discoverer of another King Tut's tomb. However, she wasn't motivated enough to study the sciences and devote the 20 years of fruitless digging first. Chellie preferred to pretend to be whatever she wanted to be, so becoming an actress was a natural. She got her BA in Dramatic Arts at the University of California Santa Barbara and went to Hollywood to become a star. She worked at Disneyland and found out that what she loved most about acting was working in small teams, and she realized she could do that in small businesses.

Working in secretarial jobs to pay rent, she got into bookkeeping. When you are focused on your mission, you are willing to do other things to support your path toward it. Chellie was amazed that she had an instinctive ability to work with numbers; it became her new fascination—even though she didn't like math in school. She joined a bookkeeping business, eventually bought her partners out, and then nearly lost the business when her key client, responsible for 75 percent of her business left suddenly. Keeping her head up, she eventually regained her financial footing and incorporated the lessons from her own financial struggles into how she worked and lived.

Chellie found that many people didn't really understand the financial statements that she was preparing for them. She spent many hours showing her clients how to read their statements and master their financial matters, and she was frequently requested to teach the subject. Suddenly, it all came together for her; her life purpose was to teach people how to manage and grow their finances with fun and ease—she loved working in small groups, with her acting background she could be entertaining, and she was talented with numbers so she was informative—her life mission came together after all these years of pursuing various aspects of it.

She dove into her life mission headfirst and started by writing and sending out flyers for the financial workshop she wanted to teach. She got zero responses, but she didn't give up; she called people up individually by phone and with her direct approach, enthusiasm and determination, she filled her first workshop.

In 1994, she gave up her bookkeeping business, and by 1995 her workshops were making her more money than she'd ever made before and she's had a six-figure annual income ever since. Chellie found her purpose and the way to fulfill it. It was not to pursue the fame and celebrity she originally imagined, but it was to be meaningful and valuable to the people that she worked with, and that is more than enough.

> If I have the belief that I can do it, I shall surely acquire the capacity to do it even if I may not have it at the beginning.
>
> —*Mahatma Gandhi*

SUDDEN AND UNEXPECTED CHANGES

Sara Davidson, the best-selling author of *Leap! What Will We Do with the Rest of Our Lives?*[8] talks about how she had to adjust when she abruptly hit the reevaluation stage, and what she had to do to regain dynamic balance and happiness. Sara was a famously successful journalist, author, TV screenwriter, and producer of hit TV shows like *Dr. Quinn, Medicine Woman*;

---

[8] Sara Davidson, *Leap! What Will We Do with the Rest of Our Lives?* (New York: Ballantine Books, 2008).

Heart Beat; *Jack and Mike*; and other shows when, in her 50s, she found herself "aged out"—regarded as too old to be in the industry any more.[9] When life dramatically shifts as in Sara's case—her work of 25 years ceased, her children went away to college, and her longtime lover left with no explanation—it is a dramatic call to reassess your life and priorities. The world as we know it has suddenly disappeared leaving us standing there with talents, tools, and rituals that seem no longer appropriate for whatever is now in front of us. It is often a frightening, lonely, and frustrating time that most of us are ill prepared for. Sara calls it the "narrows"—a hard squeeze emotionally, professionally, physically, and financially; it can severely test our belief in Spirit.

The good news is that you are not alone; everyone goes through this phase in some manner along life's journey. Some may encounter career downturns, familial rearrangements (kids, spouse, partner, etc., leaving), physical challenges (aging, illness, injury, etc.) and/or financial disruptions. Some people may experience all of them at once like Sara did. What to do when it happens? Reevaluate. It is a time to try new things. Think of it as a new opportunity to go back to the Development Stage to learn what serves you now. There is a different fit for each person. In Sara's case, she tried a variety of things—from tutoring children, to learning health and healing work, to humanitarian work in India, and living in an Indian ashram to further her spiritual pursuits—but none of them felt like her path. She felt that she was not using her gifts for the greater good.

This is a time to meditate on your life purpose, how does it apply to your current life situation? What calls to you? How can your mission guide you in your new life stage? Fortunately, Sara received a wonderful gift from our mutual friend,

---

[9] www.SaraDavidson.com

Joan Borysenko, PhD,[10] that in effect led Sara back to her life purpose. The gift was a series of questions that helped Sara realign her focus and encouraged her to develop her next phase of life.[11]

Joan Borysenko's Life Questions—Complete the Following Sentences

I realize life is both precious and short. When the angel of death comes to my door, I will be ready to go because . . .

The thing I will miss most when life is over is . . .

I have finished with . . . (name both good things and difficulties)

I still yearn to . . .

In the years to come, I will be grateful for . . .

Sara moved to Boulder, Colorado, from Hollywood, started taking piano lessons, and formed a singing trio that sings for fun, and learned how to swim. She is writing and sharing her unique perspective with the world again. After much research that included interviewing over 200 people from all over the United States, she wrote her book, *Leap! What Will We Do with The Rest of Our Lives?* so that others can learn from her experience. Her life is radically different from the fast-paced life she led in Hollywood, but she is content and happy. She says that when she reflected on what gave her happiness over the years, it was not the money and fame, as great as those were; it was the moments she spent with loved ones and the places she enjoyed. Sara is again aligned with her life purpose, to share

---

[10] www.joanborysenko.com

[11] Sara offers a free workbook on her site to help you navigate the "narrows," www.saradavidson.com/LEAP.html

and journal her experiences; ultimately, she is a chronicler of the world and that is her bliss.

To have a life mission is to have a north point in your personal compass. It will guide you and help you determine the choices you make in every aspect of your life—from career, to friends, to how you choose to spend your time, energy, and money. And your life mission is what you need to follow to bring you balance, happiness, and inner peace.

FOLLOWING YOUR LIFE PURPOSE

Jon Bon Jovi, the leader of Bon Jovi, one of the two top-grossing touring rock bands in history, worked for a while as a gofer at a radio station. His mission was to share his music with the world and by working at the radio station, he could use the recording equipment. Even with that entry into the business, it still took his band three albums and several years before they hit it big. Jon Bon Jovi had a clear idea of what he was after: to create a brand and sound for his music. As he said in an interview, he is not a rock star; he is the CEO of a multimillion-dollar corporation who has been running a brand for 25 years.[12] When you have clarity of purpose, you can move forward without being distracted by the developments along the way, whether they are unfavorable or alluring.

Janet Powers, founder of the overnight success, www.WomensToolbox.com,[13] a women's business and life online

---

[12] www.thenational.ae/arts-culture/the-visit-to-abu-dhabi-marks-the-future-for-us#full

[13] In less than four years, www.Womenstoolbox.com has reached over 20,000 unique visitors per month and has more page views per visitor than Oprah.com

network, faithfully followed her life purpose as it took her on a meandering journey. Her passion for connecting people and facilitating mutually desirable interactions guided her to change her career dramatically several times. She started her career in family planning and children's health, which led her to working with families in many developing nations around the world. Then, continuing to answer the question of how she is impacting and connecting with the world, she joined Fidelity Investments and rose to become vice president of program management, serving as the group liaison between the technical and business teams. She was making a broader connection by working on projects that were affecting thousands and even millions of lives for the better.

Still, she felt that there was a more useful way for her to fulfill her desire to bridge the gap between people. After 14 years, she left Fidelity Investments because she felt that she had something more to do; she was getting tired and the economic downturn was starting. It was time to contemplate how she was going to live the next phase of her life. She left Fidelity Investments on her own terms at age 45 to build a web design business. It was her way to build a community that would be more personally interactive again. As her web business grew, she realized how much her personal network meant to her. It was her network of family and friends that enabled her to be strong and stay the course as she leapt from one career to an uncertain future. DivaToolBox, now renamed WomensToolBox bubbled out of that aha moment; she was going to create an online community much like those that used to exist when women could easily sit down together, share their joys and concerns, and help each other. Now, just four years later, that virtual kitchen table network for women is one of the biggest in the world. Janet is happily following her life purpose to even greater impact and connection.

Your path may be like Janet's, in which you get closer with each new career to what you feel most passionate about, or it could be more like MJ Ryan's,[14] evolving as she grew. MJ's career was, as she called it, a total accident. She went with the "warmer, warmer, colder, colder" approach to her career; she kept moving toward what appealed to her and away from what didn't interest her. MJ didn't know much about the job options open to her when she graduated from college. Even though she had done well in school, she wanted to explore the world. She started work as a cashier, then as a special education aide, and then as a reporter for consumer issues for a newspaper. There she discovered editing, a profession she had never known existed before. It was like acting as a midwife to help people birth their vision.

MJ really liked editing and thought it was easy, and suddenly it dawned on her that it was okay to have a career that felt natural and fun. She dove into editing as a profession. In a relatively short time, MJ became the CEO and editorial director for Conari Press, one of the creators of the *New York Times* best-selling *Random Acts of Kindness* book series; authored many best sellers including, *The Happiness Makeover*,[15] and has over 1.75 million books in print.

After 25 years of loving what she was doing, she grew tired of her work and didn't find it interesting any more. Thinking that it was just a tough year, with a huge workload and her father dying the same year, MJ took a sabbatical to refresh herself. She wrote three more books after that but still could not revive her interest in her work. It was time for her to employ her "warmer, warmer, colder, colder" approach again to identify her next

---

[14] www.mj-ryan.com

[15] M. J. Ryan, *The Happiness Makeover* (New York: Crown Archetype, 2005).

career. She took another leave from work and gradually over a couple of years transitioned to another form of midwifery: coaching and consulting with people on how to birth their vision while continuing to be a writer and editor.

The concept of your life purpose is big and may seem far away. Think of it as a constellation that you have to squint at in order to see the overall pattern. Bring forth what is inside you at the moment and allow yourself to evolve while staying on your path. Each step is a throughway on your journey to finding your purpose.

LIFE PURPOSE, HEALTH, AND HAPPINESS

Here's more good news about living your life mission, you'll live longer[16] and keep your mental acuity sharper![17] Longitudinal studies published in *Psychosomatic Medicine* by Patricia A. Boyle, PhD, and her colleagues from the Rush Alzheimer's Disease Center show that after adjusting for age, sex, education, and race, people with a higher life purpose had a substantially reduced risk of mortality—they were 50 percent less likely to die over the follow-up period as compared to a person with no higher reason for living. And they were also able to think more clearly and have better memory than people with little higher life purpose, too! To quote Dr. Boyle, "These findings suggest that purpose in life protects against the harmful effects of plaques and tangles on memory and other thinking abilities.

[16] Patricia A. Boyle, "Having a Higher Purpose in Life Reduces Risk of Death among Older Adults," *Psychosomatic Medicine* 71 (June 2009): 574–579.

[17] Patricia A. Boyle, PhD, Rush University Medical Center, press release, "Purpose in Life May Protect against Harmful Changes in the Brain Associated with Alzheimer's Disease," May 7, 2012.

This is encouraging and suggests that engaging in meaningful and purposeful activities promotes cognitive health in old age."

How do you find your passion and life mission? First you have to trust that you have one—your own, not what others may have imprinted in your mind. Sometimes your true purpose is what you are already doing—if so, you understand and are at ease with the choices you have made in your life.

You feel happy, contented, and dedicated to your chosen life path. Sure, there are times when you are frustrated, and you may even temporarily forget why or what motivates you; that is natural for all human beings. You know who you are and what you are here on earth to do and be. Congratulations, you are one of the fortunate ones on the planet. This book will help you address the "hows" so that you can be more effective in achieving your mission.

The majority of people, however, may have some uncertainty about your life mission. Don't worry, you can determine it and develop it. Deep inside each of us there is a calling, a quest and hunger that we were born to satisfy. You can delve into your inner world and bring it out to guide your life. Here's how:

Your Heart's Prayer
Before you dedicate your life
to a person, a marriage, a family;
to a corporation, a political party, a peace campaign;
to a religion, a revolution, a spiritual path;
make one other dedication first.
First dedicate yourself to LOVE.
Decide to let Love be your intention, your purpose and
your point.
And then let Love inspire you,
support you, and guide you

in every other dedication
you make thereafter.

—Robert Holden

THE LIFE PURPOSE EXERCISE PROCESS

First find a quiet place where you feel comfortable and set aside at least 35 minutes of uninterrupted time for yourself. Have with you a pen or pencil and a writing pad. Yes, I know many of you write mostly on a computer but writing with your hand connects you more deeply to the core of your being. We are working to link you closer to your inner self. If you really have a difficult time with using paper and pen, use a computer the *next* time you do this exercise. Please, at least for the first time, use paper and pen. You will be amazed.

Sit in a comfortable chair or on a cushion and settle down mentally into your quiet space. If you meditate, utilize that process now to facilitate an open mind. If you are somewhat new to meditation, here are a few simple steps to help you clear your mind.

1. Breathe in deeply and exhale emptying your lungs gently. Keep repeating this process and with each new breath notice the air going in and coming out of your nostrils.
2. Allow your awareness to extend to the rest of your body; notice how the rest of your body feels. Where is the air going? Do you feel more circulation and warmth in your body? Center your awareness in the center of your body, a bit above your belly button. As you stay with the process you may sense your body gradually relaxing.

3. Continue breathing and observing your body's response. When a thought comes into your mind, let it go gracefully without judgment. Thoughts are going to arise; when you disregard them they will leave. It is only when we pay attention to them do they hang around.

4. Many thoughts may come and it could be a challenge to find that quiet space—keep the faith. Allow the thoughts to come and go, do not judge the thoughts or your ability to have a quiet mind. You will notice that it gets easier over time. Even long-time meditators have less than perfect sessions. Be kind to yourself, that's a large part of what this is all about!

For some of us, a repetitive physical activity like walking helps to still our minds. Mahatma Gandhi frequently went on walking meditations to complement his sitting meditations. Buddhist monk Thich Nhat Hanh developed a form of meditation based on this concept—it is named appropriately, the Walking Meditation. Find the method that best stills your mind chatter and gives you the mental spaciousness that invites your inner wisdom to surface.

When your mind is open, ask yourself the question: "What makes me happy?" Write down whatever comes to your mind. Keep writing. After the first several sentences you may find that you have some resistance—persevere and just put down whatever comes into your mind about the question. When you break through the block, deeper feelings will come through. Remember to continue to breathe deeply and stay centered in your body. Don't judge your thoughts; just jot them down. Journal for at least for 10 minutes and if you have more, continue.

Then start on the next question: "How do you want to be remembered?" Repeat the above exercise. When you feel that you have exhausted the topics for the moment, close your eyes. Sense into your body again. What are you feeling? What images are coming to your mind? Allow yourself to review them as if you are an observer. With compassion ask yourself the questions: "Is there more that you want to say to me now? Anything else that is important for me to know?" Listen carefully to the answers.

SUMMARY OF THE LIFE PURPOSE PROCESS

1. Create a quiet space for a minimum of 35 minutes.

2. Prepare pen/pencil and paper and a comfortable place to sit to journal.

3. Settle your mind—practice your meditation or try the steps described in the previous section for quieting your mind.

4. Freely jot down the thoughts that come to your mind as you ask the question: What makes me happy?

5. Write on the subject for at least 10 minutes.

6. Keep breathing and stay relaxed without judgment.

7. Ask yourself "What do I want to be remembered for?"

8. Journal on the question for at least 10 minutes.

9. Close your eyes and review the whole process—listen for the answers—write down anything that you want to add to your responses above.

Congratulations, you are now on the path to determining your life mission. Please note that this is a journey; you are in the process of uncovering something precious that may have been buried for most of your life. Whatever insights you get from the exercise will grow as you let it unfold in your mind. Repeat this process several times over the next few days and weeks until you have delved into the deepest desire you have—your very reason for being alive.

In the process of claiming your life purpose, you will also be affirming the values that you hold dearest. Your values and your mission are the foundation for your life. Nurture them; use them as your assessment tools to make decisions that will ensure you are living accordance with what is dearest to you. This will help you know when you are making the choice(s) that will lead you to where you want to be.

Each one of us was born to fulfill a destiny. When you uncover yours, initially it may be a soft resonating whisper. With nurture, it will act like your personal foghorn guiding you through any confusion and murkiness surrounding any important decision. You will find that you can see past the inevitable obstacles in life to the bigger picture of what is truly important.

Armed now with your life purpose, we are going to help you move forward to transforming your dreams into real life—the life that you are living.

> As a young man, I yearned for the day when, rooted in the experience that comes only with age, I could do my work fearlessly. But today, in my mid-60s, I realize that I will feel fear from time to time for the rest of my life. I may never get rid of my fear. But . . . I can learn to walk into it and through it whenever it rises up . . . naming the inner force that triggers . . . fear. . . . Naming our fears aloud . . . is the first step toward transcending them.
>
> —*Parker J. Palmer*

4

ONE STEP
AT A TIME

One step at a time is good walking.

—Chinese proverb

You're ready to do something about the overload and stress in your life; the question is where do you start?

There may be more than one aspect of your life causing you discomfort and anxiety—this is common in today's taxing world. Oftentimes, the sore points are related to each other and aggravating other areas of your life. Whew, what does this mean? It just means that you are human and living in our modern hyperspeed world—just recognizing and acknowledging the situation is a step toward improving it.

Many years ago when I was vice president of Nike, I lived in Lake Oswego, Oregon, while my husband stayed in Southern California for his work. Both of our jobs were exciting, very taxing, and could suck up all the time there was in each day and more. After nine months of long-distance commuting, we were both tired and cranky when we saw each other. Our visions of enjoying our precious time together went out the window soon after we reunited because we were both worn out from the stress of working long, pressure-filled days. Packing up and flying during the little free time we had to see each other and then having to pack up again after a day made our times together less than relaxing. We argued over petty little things and felt unappreciated by each other. It seemed that our relationship was breaking down.

Our physical and mental health was also affected. We didn't exercise as much as we used to since we were jamming all the demands of a week into five days so that we could be together the other two. When our physical body is out of sync, our mental health is also affected. Laundry, household chores, grocery shopping, bills, and all the other demands of daily life somehow still had to be dealt with, while more important things were calling for our attention. Piles of papers and unfinished tasks lying around reminded me of what I still had to do—it made me feel miserably inept. I felt especially bad when a friend or, even worse, my husband or his children from a previous marriage would ask me for something, and I couldn't respond in a timely fashion. My work was demanding and exciting; learning a new industry, company culture, and town/living arrangement while developing a comprehensive and innovative new strategy for an emerging apparel division for one of the world's largest athletic company was a tall order. I was being stretched so thin that I didn't even recognize that I was stretched thin!

I even contemplated spending more time at work and foregoing more of our personal time because the work was so challenging. One visit around New Year's resulted in my husband leaving early to go back to California in a huff. It finally struck us that our priorities were out of order. It took that big of a jolt for us to realize that our work had taken over our lives.

Have you ever been there? You have so much on your plate that you are not even aware of the enormity of the problem. In many ways that is easy to do—we add one more thing to our lists of to-dos or ought-to-dos and we soldier on. The last obligation we took on may be a good or necessary one, but we never stopped to review and assess if there was anything or even several other things we could take off our plate.

> We need to maintain a proper balance in our life by allocating the time we have. There are occasions where saying no is the best time management practice there is.
> —*Catherine Pulsife*

I have too much to do! I need a day stretcher! Where does the time go? I admit I've said those very words myself, and more than once. To get everything that you most value done is about prioritizing and managing our expectations and, consequently, our time to best use. Remembering my life mission and taking a moment (or more) to center myself is how I come back into dynamic balance and realize what I cherish most are my relationships. With that in mind I make the choices that determine how and what I am going to do next.

Here's some good news, we all have the same 24 hours a day—there is no one with more or less time. That means Mozart (died at 35 years old), Michelangelo (88 years old), and Shakespeare (52 years old) had exactly the same time you have. If they could accomplish their amazing work with the same 24 hours in their days, you, too, can do what you need to do. The question is how can you better utilize your time to ensure that what you most value gets done?

Here's a little quiz to help you determine where to begin the whittling process—and the good news is that you already have the right answers. All you have to do is use your life purpose, which you affirmed in the last chapter, as your guide and answer from your heart, and your priorities will be revealed.

QUALITY OF LIFE QUIZ

Rank and write about the quality of the following aspects of your life:

1. Your body
2. Relationships
3. Money and other means of exchange
4. Spiritual life
5. Your community

Similar to how you identified and affirmed your life purpose in the last chapter, use the journaling technique to figure out your next steps. I am outlining the journaling process here again for your convenience.

SUMMARY OF THE JOURNALING PROCESS

1. Create a quiet space for a minimum of 35 minutes.

2. Prepare pen/pencil and paper and a comfortable place to sit to journal.

3. Settle your mind—practice your meditation or use the quiet-the-mind technique outlined in Chapter 3.

4. Freely jot down the thoughts that come to your mind as you think about each aspect of your life as listed above.

5. Rank and write on each topic for at least five minutes.

6. Keep breathing and stay relaxed without judging your feelings and thoughts.

7. Close your eyes and mentally review the whole process— listen for the answers—write down anything that you want to add to your responses above.

To a large extent, the various aspects of your life are interrelated. Please respond by focusing on each facet to determine which one(s) are triggering discontent and problems in the other areas. Journal on each attribute and write down your feelings and thoughts about them one by one, for example:

1. Your body: "I'm overall pretty healthy but I am tired a lot and get neck pain and headaches. My health issues seem to

come mostly during the week and on Sunday night. I wonder if my neck pain, headaches, and tiredness come from my frustration at work where I am struggling to stay interested in what I do. It seems so meaningless as I have been doing the same thing for so long and it doesn't seem to make a difference. . . . "

That response is a composite of the remarks I've heard from people I've coached. In this example, they are saying that even though their physical health may have some challenges, the underlying cause seems to stem from their dissatisfaction at work. When they rank and write about their work, this knowledge of the reason for their health issues will help them identify what is frustrating about their work. With new insight, they can explore what they can do to improve their work situation so that all aspects of their lives are more in balance. For people with this profile, it would be most effective to start by reviewing their career and analyze what they are drawn to and what they wish to modify. They can then make plans to start the process of changing it.

Go over all the different aspects of your life and rank them and write about your satisfaction or dissatisfaction with them. When you are done, go back and read them again, add any further thoughts you have about each area.

Now draw a simple circle to represent your entire amount of time and energy, and then divide the circle into pie-shaped pieces the approximate size that you are allocating to each aspect of your life: your body, relationships, money and other means of exchange, spiritual life, and your community. No editing please. Make the wedges the real size instead of what you want them to be. How does it feel to see where you spend your time and energy as compared to how you value that sector of your life?

Just as your car runs more smoothly and requires less energy to go faster and farther when the wheels are in perfect alignment, you perform better when your thoughts, feelings, emotions, goals, and values are in balance.

—*Brian Tracy*

When you have identified the relative balance/imbalance in the various facets of your life, then you are able to make adjustments that will help you come back into balance. Look at your list and your pie chart—one or two areas will show up as where you focus most of your energy, and one or two others will be the most neglected. Before you jump in and make any drastic changes, measure these areas against your life mission that you identified in the last chapter. Is your life as you are living it now aligned with your life purpose? If so, congratulations. If not, fine-tune your energy, time, and other resources to reflect more of a balance in your life. Pay more attention to the areas most overlooked and dial back on the most heavily emphasized ones.

When I speak about balance I mean *dynamic balance*. At different times in our lives, our priorities vary. Life is active and constantly changing, as do our needs at different stages. It is unrealistic and almost impossible, as well as unnecessary, to allocate the same amount of energy and resources to every aspect of your life. Each person has individual wants and needs that ebb and flow over time. Therefore, balance is dynamic. What is right and comfortable for you at 25 is most probably radically different from what is suitable and comfortable for you when you are 45 or 50. You have to be aware and reassess and adjust your dynamic balance as your life situation changes. What doesn't change is your life mission, which is your constant guide and the north point of your personal life compass. Use your life purpose as the criteria to assess your quality of life at various times in your life.

Most of us have unbalanced areas that are screaming for help and attention at every stage in life—that is a by-product of our natural life cycle changes. The relentless pace of life today heightens the intensity of discomfort and amount of change needed. Knowing your life purpose will help guide you in allocating the proper amount of energy and attention to each aspect of your life. Dynamic balance is what we strive for—we can't do it all but we can adjust the resources we dedicate toward each part of our life at each particular period. By being conscious about what we choose to do, we can get buy-in and cooperation from others more easily than when we are acting without awareness. We can make purposeful decisions and plans once we are conscious of our true values instead of reacting to outside events.

> The best and safest thing is to keep a balance in your life, acknowledge the great powers around us and in us. If you can do that, and live that way, you are really a wise man.
>
> —*Euripides*

Recently, some fascinating findings about what keeps people healthy and living a long and happy life were released. A longevity research project tracked 1,500 people from childhood to old age and death started in 1921 and is still ongoing. Howard S. Friedman, PhD, and Leslie R. Martin, PhD, published the results of this eight-decade study in their book, *The Longevity Project*. The results are enlightening:

> The people who worked the hardest lived the longest. Being involved in, committed to, and successful at work is an excellent predictor of health and longevity.
>
> Social relations are important to good health, but it didn't much matter if you felt appreciated; much more important

was how much social involvement you had with other people each day.

Staying active in middle age was more important than being active or being an athlete in youth. In fact, if you gradually became more physically active as you aged, that was a very good sign.

Happiness is related to health but not because laughter clears clogged arteries. Rather, we found that the same kinds of meaningful and consequential lives that promoted health also promoted happiness.[1]

As you review your priorities, chew on this information. What is of consequence to life is to create meaning, have social interactions that you value, and to nurture your physical body. In my consulting work with high potential corporate and nonprofit leaders and in my own life, I find that one is most alive, healthy and successful when one is making a positive difference; taking care of himself or herself physically, mentally, and spiritually; and has loving relationships. You now know your life purpose and your priorities; seize the moment, take the steps to gain your dynamic balance and the life you've always dreamed of. You can start now!

The next few chapters focus on the decision points in your life. Look over your responses to the quality of life quiz and match them against the chapters—Money, Relationships, Spirit, Body, Your Community—which one do you want to deal with first? It may not be the most out of balance one; choose to read about the one that you are most interested in working on now. Wherever you want to begin is perfect, every

---

[1] Howard S. Friedman, and Leslie R. Martin, *The Longevity Project: Surprising Discoveries for Health and Long Life from the Landmark Eight-Decade Study* (New York: Hudson Street Press, 2011).

aspect is interrelated, and when you work on one the others are improved in the process. Congratulations, you are already making solid steps to more happiness.

Wherever you are is the entry point.

—Rumi

5

MONEY AND OTHER MEANS OF EXCHANGE

What we really want to do is what we are really meant to do. When we do what we are meant to do, money comes to us, doors open for us, we feel useful, and the work we do feels like play to us.

—*Julia Cameron*

Money is the root of all evil. Money makes the world go round. We've heard both of these statements and maybe even said them ourselves. And neither is completely true. Of course money is useful to have, and it sure makes getting things done much easier. Money, as powerful as it can be, is not the final determinant of the well-being of the world and in one's life. Nor does money control how happy we are. How do we use money wisely and cope with our fear of its lack?

Our mental conditioning and feelings about money are rooted in how the people around us dealt with money when we were young. We generally either took on their perspective or completely rejected it and embraced the opposite. The awareness of this fact may already be obvious to us, but more relevant is how can we apply that knowledge to improve our lives now? The actual amount of money we have is oftentimes secondary to how we view money—just ask any 5-year-old kid with $20 in a candy store how he or she feels and then ask an adult that same question when he or she is looking at the menu of a fine restaurant with only $20 in their wallet! Our expectations, values, and goals drive the way we view and handle money and our pursuit of it.

How do we differentiate our own feelings about money from what society markets to us incessantly? We are bombarded with messages that tell us if we are rich, we are smart, funny, good-looking, have the right partner, are well respected, free to do whatever we want, and of course, we are happy. With that message being communicated to us in numerous ways, it is easy to understand why many of us believe that money does, indeed, buy happiness. And worse yet, you cannot be happy if you don't have lots of money.

Money and its common cultural extensions of property, cars, expensive clothes, jewelry, and so on, and the social status most people attribute to individuals with money, is a big factor in how we think, handle our daily affairs, our careers, and who we interact with and how. Money is energy, like electricity or fire. It can be used for good or ill. It is up to us to apply and channel money to serve us. We are not run or held hostage by it. I repeat: money is our servant.

I'm not saying that money is a negative. It can do an amazing amount of good and facilitate getting many things accomplished. There is a difference between barely surviving and thriving. Where that line is differs for each person. Working in India with Vitamin Angels[1] to distribute vitamins to malnourished and undernourished children, I witnessed what people in the West would consider impossible conditions. Entire families subsisted on less than 40 rubles a day—less than a dollar a day! I was oftentimes the tallest and fattest person present, and given that I am less than 5-foot 5-inches tall and about 110 pounds, that is a sad indication of the amount of food and nutrients available. Health care? There is essentially none aside from what people could do for themselves. They are maintaining life as well as they know how and have their joys and contentment, too. Could they be happier with more food and other basics of life? Absolutely!

And I've spent time with people who have several hundred thousands of dollars a year in income who feel constrained and fraught with anxiety because they worry that they don't have enough. It may be easy to judge such people and say that they

---

[1] Vitamin Angels, www.vitaminangels.org

should look at others with much less. Yet, for them to maintain their work, their children's education, and the acquisition of material goods that is expected in the social circles they travel, it takes a certain amount of money, and from their perspective, yes, they do need more.

So there is a balance. How do you choose to spend your life? What is your life mission? What makes you happy? Those are the questions we have to answer truthfully to find happiness. Your life mission will guide you. Once we have achieved the basics of life there is a wide range of choices for us to pick from to determine if we are happy and at peace.

Many people also have issues with money and personal worth. In today's world, many people's self-worth is tied to how much people are willing to pay for their work. And we know the fallacy of that, too—look at the wild insecurities of exorbitantly paid celebrities, which are played out in the media frequently. Do you value your work? Women, especially, have a hard time asking for the appropriate amount of money for their work. This is reflected in the pay disparity between women and men for similar work. Generally women are paid 23 percent less for doing the same work that men do.[2] Are you comfortable setting the proper price for what you do? Do some research into comparables and determine a fair market value for your skills. With your increasing personal confidence in your own worth, you will perform better and garner the proper reward for your work.

Being aware of the tangled emotional webs money weaves over us is the start of learning how we can unravel the ties. We

---

[2] Women's earnings were 77.4 percent of men's in 2010, compared to 77.0 percent in 2009, according to Census statistics released September 13, 2011, based on the median earnings of all full-time, year-round workers. Fifty years ago women earned 61 percent of what men earned.

can then consciously decide how we choose to use money and other forms of exchange to achieve our life mission. We will be free to actively pursue the path we choose in our career, friends, the goods and services we buy, where we live, and so on. It's absolutely liberating and joyful!

Remember, you have absolute control over three things in your life:

1. The thoughts you think.
2. The images you visualize.
3. The actions you take (including what you say to others).

—*Jack Canfield*

If you want to make a million you don't have to understand money, what you have to understand is people's fears about money.

—*William Gaddis*

How to Make Money

Chellie Campbell is a Financial Stress Reduction expert;[3] she coaches people who have issues with money for a living. Her advice to people who have fears or conflicts about money comes from experiencing and learning from them herself. She believes that you should indeed make lots of money and you will once you identify the mental restrictions that are holding you back. In Chapter 3, Chellie shared her story of going from bankruptcy to regaining her financial footing to now making

---

[3] www.chelliecampbell.com

more money than she's ever had in her life by doing what makes her the happiest.

Her eight points to achieving financial comfort and freedom are simple and effective.

CHELLIE CAMPBELL'S EIGHT STEPS TO FINANCIAL FREEDOM

1. **The Power of Positive Thinking**
   Stop thinking of the potential doom and gloom—you are either working in fear or in faith. Fear is just faith in bad things happening, shift your thinking to believing good things are developing for you. Your attitude will show in every way—body language, speech, and all your thoughts. She says, "fake it till you make it." Reframe what you are doing in a positive light, for example, think that you are offering to help people who need you instead of making sales calls. When you see favorable results from your efforts you will gain confidence and feel more encouraged. You begin to develop a positive feedback loop.

2. **Send Out Ships**
   In the 1800s, investors would send ships off to trade for goods for months and even years at a time, eventually some of the ships came back laden with amazing bounty and riches. This is where the saying, "waiting for my ship to come in," referring to the long awaited arrival of great wealth and reward, comes from. You have to send out many ships (ideas, projects, inquires, etc.) because some of them may encounter problems and not return. You are in charge of shipping out your efforts and doing your best to ensure their success, but you are not in charge of when or if they come in. Visualize and plan for them to come back to you overflowing with what you want.

3. **Count Your Money**

Make a budget; you need to know how much you have to spend and save. Without a budget you may overspend in an area and not be able to manage in others. A budget is your friend—it stands for Baby U Deserve Getting Every Thing!

4. **Manage Your Time**

Prioritize your time and spend it effectively so you can achieve the proper balance to finance your life. Plan your work/career so that you have enough time for all the most important things in your life. As an example, she explained that she chose to teach small-group workshops instead of individual coaching so that she can make similar income with fewer working hours.

5. **Goal Getting, Not Goal Setting**

Analyze your circumstances. What do you have to do now to get what you want? Keep your mission in mind and you can work through the current situation.

6. **Breakthrough**

Breakthrough usually comes after breakdown—you have to work through the rejections and problems before you get to the breakthrough. Survive the storms and you will arrive at the successful, happy, sunshiny day!

7. **Swim with Dolphins and Avoid the Sharks and Tunas**

Stay the course—you have to reach "your people" and avoid "not your people." You can't please everyone—it's impossible—you have to be you. When you are authentically you then people who will like you will be attracted to you. Dolphins are happy and honest; sharks are only out for themselves, and tunas are the victims who are wishing harder than working.

8. **Live in the Present and Be Happy**

Keep your inner peace—remember your life purpose. Your goal in life is to be happy. Ask yourself: If everyone in the world thought the way you think, what would the world be like? Use that as a gauge as to whether you are on track to where you want to be. The purpose of life is to enjoy it, and help others do the same!

I love money. I love everything about it. I bought some pretty good stuff. Got me a $300 pair of socks. Got a fur sink. An electric dog polisher. A gasoline powered turtleneck sweater. And, of course, I bought some dumb stuff, too.

—*Steve Martin*

MONEY AND YOUR LIFE MISSION

Howard Schiffer was living the good life. He was making a comfortable income, his wife and son were both doing well, and they lived in a lovely home in Santa Barbara, California. One day he heard about a game from a friend in which people would write their own obituaries. As he pondered on this strange idea an uneasy feeling came to him; he realized that at that point in his life if he were to die, people would probably say about him: "He sold a lot of products." Feeling acutely uncomfortable with that legacy, Howard decided he needed to change his life.

The amount of money he made, and the financial security that his career afforded him, wasn't as important as what he felt he needed to do to feed his soul. Just being in business wasn't enough. Something was pulling at him; he *had* to change course. He knew he had so much more to give; he wanted to find out what he could do to give his life a deeper meaning. Howard got into the supplements and vitamin business because of his passion for health and helping others. His speaking coach would tell him that everyone's life is a laboratory designed to create one thing; he was now looking to find his one thing. Howard's life mission is to make the best use of the life he's been given by connecting with people and helping them. He's had several careers already, from midwifery and prenatal education, to the natural health industry and being an entrepreneur. How was he going combine these all into something more impactful?

Knowing how critical the proper vitamins are for a developing child, Howard decided to combine all his experiences and contacts in the prenatal education, entrepreneurial, and nutritional supplements industries into providing vitamins to chronically malnourished and undernourished children and mothers worldwide. He started his vision, Vitamin Angels Alliance,[4] in his bedroom, first as a supplemental business with a partner and eventually as a stand-alone nonprofit. Initially working only with volunteers, he didn't draw a salary or have any health insurance benefits for the first 10 years. He did consulting work in the natural products industry, dabbled in mergers and acquisitions, and started another business to pay the bills. He also wrote and published three books and maxed out both a second mortgage on his house and a personal line of credit to keep everything going.

Money was a tool; he used it to achieve his life purpose. Working day and night to support his mission and his family,

---

[4] www.VitaminAngels.org

he was nevertheless happier and more at peace than he'd ever been.

Now 18 years later, Vitamin Angels, which started as a dream in Howard's bedroom, is now helping 25 million children in 40 countries around the world. In 2006, the World Bank assembled a group of 50 world-class economists, called the Copenhagen Consensus, to analyze and determine the best solutions to the world's greatest global development challenges. Micronutrient supplementation (specifically vitamin A) for malnourished and undernourished children was ranked as the number one priority. Howard's vision of what he can do to make the best use of his life was prescient. He considers the work with Vitamin Angels a blessing and is thankful for all the amazing people who have helped to make it a reality. His obituary is now in line with the vision he had for his life. He is indeed making the best use of the life he has been given.

Howard is now happily thriving, making a living, and looking toward a time when Vitamin Angels will be seen as the go-to organization for supplement interventions, serving the most vulnerable and difficult to reach in the world. Is he making as much money as he could have had he stayed in his former career? No. Is he content and more at peace than ever before? A resounding yes! He is richly compensated in the joy, love, and growing health of all the children and moms he has been able to help. How and how much money you make is a choice. The choice comes down to what and how you choose to live your life mission—you have to do what makes you happy. But if you ask Howard, he would say that starting Vitamin Angels was not a choice. In his words, "I knew I wouldn't have a life unless I did this. I honestly *had* to do Vitamin Angels in order to save myself as much as the children we would be reaching."

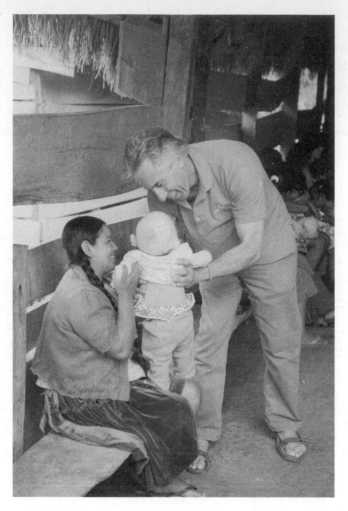

Howard Schiffer, founder and president of Vitamin Angels on location in Bolivia sharing a moment with a mother and child and on nutrition and critical micronutrient supplements

Source: photo©Vitamin Angels / Matt Dayka. For more photos and information of the all experts in the book, please go to www.MarilynTam.com.

Yes, it is absolutely fine, and in fact fun to enjoy money! It is a tool and we are free to use it to our best benefit. Howard loves how he chose to deal with money; he has raised and continues to bring in a vast amount of resources for Vitamin Angels. His personal needs with Vitamin Angels revolve more around the satisfaction and joy he receives from seeing the smiles and the physical and cognitive improvements in the children and parents that Vitamin Angels have helped. Howard says, "Whatever I've put into Vitamin Angels, I've gotten back a hundredfold. Having a child reach up to hold my hand in some remote village—their way of saying thank-you for not forgetting us—is more than I could have ever expected." That gives Howard the most happiness; this is the form of exchange that truly pays him for his work—and that is his choice. You may choose differently; this is the magic in viewing and using money; you have a choice.

> Often people attempt to live their lives backwards, they try to have more things or more money in order to do more of what they want so that they will be happier. The way it actually works is the reverse. You must first be who you really are then do what you need to do in order to have what you want.
>
> —*Margaret Young*

"MONEY DOESN'T TALK, IT SWEARS"

Mark Albion, PhD, author of the *New York Times* best seller *Making a Life, Making a Living*, and the co-founder of More than Money Careers[5] has another perspective on money. Quoting Bob Dylan, he says, "Money doesn't talk, it swears." Money is critical to survival and although it is easy to pooh-pooh the importance of money, it is deeply lodged in our

---

[5] Mark Albion, http://morethanmoneycareers.com/

psyche. Mark's father regarded money as the measure of whether Mark was successful and, indeed, whether he was even a man. According to his religion, Judaism, Mark says, a person who is wealthy can be a good person, as well. For example, Abraham, the father of three major religions—Christianity, Islam, and Judaism—was a wealthy man and a good man. God's test is how one makes his money and what he does with it—that is, whether a person makes and uses money to create a world of more social and economic justice.

How we feel about money is deeply embedded in our consciousness and subconsciousness; we have to truly examine and align our inner feelings about money before we are able to utilize all our energies in concert to achieve what we desire. What we don't know can sabotage our efforts. Mark followed the track his family, religion, and culture put him on and became a respected and well-compensated Harvard Business School professor. He was living the good life of affluence when he felt there was still something missing. Reflecting on his own inner conflicts and those of his students led him to change his life and leave Harvard.

Becoming well-known publicly in the mid-1980s for his stand on business and social values,[6] Mark began receiving suicide notes from students at top business schools who wanted to make more than money with their careers and felt like outcasts at their business schools. It was another nudge for Mark toward his decision to devote his life to what he values more—a life of dynamic balance and happiness. He has since devoted his life to helping others find their life purpose, which ultimately is what makes us happy and increases our chances of being financially prosperous. Mark's company, More Than

---

[6] Mark Albion was profiled in two *60 Minutes* shows and many other major media for his work on business and social responsibility.

Money Careers,[7] is helping students and alums bring their talents to well-paying work where they can find productive and satisfying ways of creating social and economic value. This is his dream: to cocreate a movement and ecosystem that enables talented young people to work on meaningful social challenges as an intrinsic part of their profitable careers. It's a win-win-win for all involved.

He shared the four questions from the film, Don Juan DeMarco, that he lives by now:

1. What is sacred?
2. Of what is spirit made?
3. What is worth living for?
4. What is dying for?

The only answer to all four questions to him is love.

> Being rich is having money; being wealthy is having time.
> —*Margaret Bonnano*

TIME AND MONEY

"Time is money"—we've all heard that before, and, indeed, time is equally powerful if not more so than money. How do we look at time? As a trade-off to money? Or as the equalizing factor in all life? We all have the same amount of time so it is up to us how we allocate it. With your understanding of your life mission, you can weigh the various options on how to use your time to bring you the most happiness.

---

[7] Mark Albion, http://morethanmoneycareers.com

OCED, the Organisation for Economic Co-operation and Development (36 member nations), notes that the United States is the only developed nation without a federal vacation policy.[8] The United States is the only developed country that does not require that companies give their full-time employees paid time off. A majority of U.S. workers, especially the higher paid ones, get 12 paid holidays a year,[9] but many don't take them all. Is it because we simply have too much to do and can't leave for even a few days? Or is it that we fear that our jobs will not be there when we come back? Or both?

The United States is the most productive nation in the world.[10] Should we assess whether we are happier because we are busy producing more stuff or would we be happier if we had more time to enjoy other aspects of life? Interestingly Norway, which is ranked the second happiest nation in OCED's survey,[11] is also the second most productive country in the world. And its workers get 27 paid days off as compared to the United States' unofficial 12 days.

Where does the United States rank in happiness? OCED ranks it in 11th place for happiness and number one for productivity. What is more important to us as individuals and as a country? Being the most productive or having the best life satisfaction? I maintain that we can have both—when we are happier we will also be more productive. If Norway can rank second in both, we have a good example to learn from. Along with their high degree of social benefit and time off, they are building strong economic output.

---

[8] www.law.harvard.edu/programs/lwp/papers/No_Holidays.pdf

[9] Paper by Rebecca Ray and John Schmitt for the European Commission, www.law.harvard.edu/programs/lwp/papers/No_Holidays.pdf

[10] International Labor Organization Key Indicators of the Labor Market (KILM), http://kilm.ilo.org/2011/download/kilm17EN.pdf

[11] http://247wallst.com/2012/05/22/the-happiest-countries-in-the-world-2

We can start reviewing our own personal allocation of time and energy and adjust it so that we are happy and effective. We can be dynamically balanced—choosing to make money and create a happy life, too. Use your life mission as your guide and you will get there. Mark Albion, Joan Borysenko, Chellie Campbell, Jack Canfield, Howard Schiffer, and the other experts in the book have found their life purpose; let them be the inspiration for you to find yours. What that looks like is up to you. We are rooting for you to live your happiest life!

> When I chased after money, I never had enough. When I got my life on purpose and focused on giving of myself and everything that arrived into my life, then I was prosperous.
>   —*Wayne Dyer*

6

RELATIONSHIPS

If we are incapable of finding peace in ourselves, it is pointless
to search elsewhere.

—Francois de la Rochefoucauld

We are social beings. We live in community and depend
on others to perform countless functions to make our
work and lives operate smoothly. And yet, oftentimes we feel
disassociated from others and even may think that we can do it
alone. The truth is we need meaningful relationships to thrive.
Yet we fight it—we crave togetherness and we also lament the
pain, frustration, and anger (all really just different aspects of
the same thing) that unmet expectations and disagreements in
relationships provoke in us. These emotions sometimes drive
us to the point that we swear off ever being in one again. Yes,
even the relationships we have with our parents, children,
lover, spouse, and dear friends are called into question and
sometimes broken temporarily or permanently for the rest of
our lives. After isolating ourselves for a while, most of us try
again with new people or the same one(s) from before. The
longing for connection, nurture, and meaning that relationships can bring, draw us back like a powerful magnet, indeed it
is our instinct.

You yourself, as much as anybody in the entire universe,
deserve your love and affection.

—Buddha

YOUR RELATIONSHIP WITH YOURSELF

Katherine Woodward Thomas, psychotherapist and the best-selling author of *Calling in "the One,"*[1] points out that the most important relationship we have is with ourselves. We can't be in a good relationship with anyone else if we don't have a good relationship with ourselves first. In relationships with others, we act out our subconscious feelings about ourselves. Unless we have resolved our early childhood patterning, we will most likely repeat it. For how we were treated as a child is often internalized, and now it is how we see ourselves. For instance, if we were dismissed as a child and haven't dealt with what we made that mean, we will predictably act in ways that are dismissive toward ourselves and others.

If we find ourselves feeling invisible in our relationships rather than simply getting angry and resentful that our partner is or seems to be inconsiderate of our needs, we would be wise to try to identify the negative feelings in ourselves first and resolve them so that we are happy with who we are. This will empower us to be able to establish healthy relationships with others.

But how can something that happened so many years ago still be hampering the adult you from having good relationships? Katherine explains that the wounding, the hurt didn't happen that many years ago, we are doing the same thing to ourselves now, maybe only 30 minutes ago! If our caregivers were critical, we are probably even more critical toward ourselves now, reprimanding ourselves for our perceived inadequacies and failures and stingy with approval and praise for ourselves and others.

---

[1] Katherine Woodward Thomas, *Calling in "The One"* (New York: Three Rivers Press, 2004).

Changing our self-image is often easier said than done. We can talk about the old patterns and even use them as an excuse to behave a certain way; *"I was told I was no good when I was young, so now I need more positive feedback because I was badly wounded as a child."* I've heard versions of this many times while I'm coaching adults, often said as if their history gives them the right to more consideration and goodies now.

From as young as I can remember, my mother regularly told me that I was a waste of a pregnancy and emphasized her point with physical beatings. I understand how it feels to be told that one is not good enough. It burns into your heart and there is a helpless feeling that no matter what you do you cannot make them happy.

That hunger for approval and the hopelessness of the quest can grind down and destroy your self-confidence and self-image. However, we are not children any more; we can make other choices and choose other thoughts. Whoever caused you pain may never change, but you can. Step inside their shoes; what conditioning and background did they have to make them act that way? That is not to say that their behavior is acceptable, just learn to understand so that you can release the resentment and the expectation that they could have done better. Let go of that old burden of judgment, forgive, and move on. You will feel much lighter, more empowered, like yourself more, and see the world in a better light once you do.

> To forgive is to set a prisoner free and discover that the prisoner was you.
>
> —*Lewis B. Smedes*

Robin Casarjian is the founder and director of LionHeart Foundation,[2] a nonprofit organization that counsels and

---

[2] www.lionheart.org/

educates prisoners, and works with highly at-risk youth and teen parents on how to make different choices so that they do not land in jail. She wrote a book on forgiveness[3] to help people deal with the anger, resentment, desire for revenge, and other emotions that bind the victim to the perpetrator. She says that the bitterness and rage that people carry with them is hurting themselves the most. Forgiveness liberates the forgiver; we forgive for our own good. Forgiveness is not condoning the acts or the persons; you don't have to bring them into your life now. You can move on with your life with greater freedom and happiness after you forgive them.

Look at Nelson Mandela. He was jailed and confined to a small uninsulated cell, the floor was his bed, a bucket his toilet, he was forced to do hard labor in a rock quarry daily. He was allowed one visitor a year for 30 minutes. He could write and receive one letter every six months.[4] After enduring 27 years in these horrific prison conditions, he was finally released. And yet for his inauguration as the first black president of South Africa, he invited his jailer to be his VIP guest. Forgiveness frees the forgiver. There are many stories of people who endured heart-wrenching pain and suffering who later forgive their perpetrators, and in that transformation they were both transported to a much healthier place. Let Nobel Peace Prize Laureate Desmond Tutu share the story of how South Africa came to heal the horrors of apartheid:

> Our country chose a middle way of individual amnesty for truth. Some would say, what about justice? And we say retributive justice is not the only kind of justice. There is

---

[3] Robin Casarjian, *Forgiveness: A Bold Choice for a Peaceful Heart* (New York: Bantam, 1992).

[4] www.pbs.org/wgbh/pages/frontline/shows/mandela/prison/

also restorative justice, because we believe in Ubuntu—the essence of being human, that idea that we are all caught up in a delicate network of interdependence. We say, "A person is a person through other persons." I need you in order to be me and you need me in order to be you. The greatest good is communal corporate harmony, and resentment, anger, revenge are corrosive of this harmony. To nurse grudges and resentment is bad for your blood pressure. Psychologists have now found that to forgive is good for our personal, physical, psychic health, as well as our health as a community, as a society. We discovered that people experienced healing through telling their stories. The process opened wounds that were festering. We cleansed them, poured ointment on them, and knew they would heal. A young man who had been blinded by police action in his township came to tell us the story of that event. When he finished he was asked how he felt now, and he said, "You have given me back my eyes." Retribution leads to a cycle of reprisal, leading to counter-reprisal in an inexorable movement, as in Rwanda, Northern Ireland, and in the former Yugoslavia. The only thing that can break that cycle, making possible a new beginning, is forgiveness. Without forgiveness there is no future.[5]

It is one thing to know that one needs to forgive and another thing to actually do it. What I have found works well in forgiving is understanding that each person is doing the best they can from whatever conditioning and perspective that they have. It takes the "shoulds" out of our mind and allows the acceptance of what was. The person(s) who blinded the young man in South Africa did it out of their own fears, which provoked the anger and violence they perpetuated on him.

---

[5] www.sol.com.au/kor/19_03.htm

My mother acted out of her own conditioning that girls are not desirable. It is not to say that they were right. It is to say that whatever caused them to think the way that they did motivated their actions. They were doing the best they knew how from what they know.

Whether others ever change is not something I can control. The only person I can change is me. I can demand retributive justice, or like the country of South Africa, choose restorative justice. Their belief in *Unbuntu*, that the well-being of each person is linked to everyone else's and that clinging to past hurts damages the person clutching onto them, helped the entire country move forward from the numerous horrors of apartheid. For me, my goal is to be free of all burdens that weigh me down. Holding onto anger, resentment, and the desire for redress is taxing and wearying. Are you ready to be free and have more energy and less inner chatter?

Take the time and effort to heal those wounds. Seek help from a therapist or other trained professional. Or, if you are ready and comfortable, you can do as you did in finding your life purpose; set aside at least 35 minutes of quiet time to reflect and journal on the process. Like South Africa, you can open up the festering sores, clean them, and allow them to heal.

If you choose to release the bitterness yourself, you can use the journaling process, as discussed in Chapter 3, Life Purpose—Yours. After you take the time to still your mind and center yourself, write a letter from the person(s) or group(s) that you are holding a judgment against to yourself. Imagine that you are in their skin. How do they feel? Why do they think the way they do? Write from their perspective as to why they did what they did.

At first it may seem completely impossible to even imagine how anyone could behave the way they did. You may feel frustration, fear, or anger. Recognize that you are safe where you are and breathe through it. If it is too intense, continue to do deep breaths. It is only when we avoid the pain that it seems unbearable; when we allow it to be, it will wash over us and dissipate. We can observe where it hurts in our body and mind and realize that we are not in the originating situation any more. We have a choice to take other action and think other thoughts. Continue to breathe and watch your own reactions.

When you are ready, write again, why did they do what they did? Journal until you have an understanding of their motivations—you do not have to agree with them at all. Just understand. From that place of understanding you will have a sense of compassion, that the perpetrators, too, are victims of their conditions. Release them and take back the power you gave them by allowing them free space in your mind. Thank them—and yourself—in your mind for the lesson. Hug yourself and tell yourself how proud you are that you are courageous enough to truthfully examine these old wounds. You can revisit this process again as you feel the need and for now, be happy that you took another step in letting go of the past that was binding you.

The relationship we have with ourselves has to be strong and stable enough to serve as the foundation to build on and to fulfill our potential for creativity and greatness. Forgiveness liberates our energy from being used to hold onto grudges and resentment so that we can use all our energy for productive and enjoyable things.

> When you hold resentment toward another, you are bound
> to that person or condition by an emotional link that is
> stronger than steel. Forgiveness is the only way to dissolve
> that link and get free.
>
> —*Katherine Ponder*

Katherine Woodward Thomas shared that in her work with thousands of people, she has found that our relationships with others are merely a mirror of the relationship we have with ourselves. If we don't pay attention to our own needs and emotions we draw the same dynamic into our relationships—it takes a conscious interrelationship to change that. If we are only outwardly focused on what is wrong with our relationships, we are doomed to failure and continuing unhappiness.[6]

> Your task is not to seek for love, but merely to seek and find all the barriers within yourself that you have built against it.
>
> —*Rumi*

In Katherine's Feminine Power[7] work with teaching partner, Claire Zammit they developed a course to help us evolve beyond these old patterns and to have happy, healthy, thriving relationships with others. Here are the three steps they established on how to move out of that vicious cycle of blame and resentment into healthy, happy relationships.[8]

1. Create a loving and generative relationship with yourself in order to evolve beyond your old story and begin living from the deeper truth of who you are and what is possible for you. To resolve these old issues from childhood, Katherine suggests that you put aside analysis and the search for intellectual understanding of your feelings. Focus instead on the relationship between the mature, adult part of you and the younger part of you that is holding the old limiting

---

[6] http://callingintheone.com/

[7] www.femininepower.com

[8] Additional material, coaching and workshops are available from Katherine Woodward Thomas, http://callingintheone.com/

story about yourself, created in response to what happened to you when you were young. Feel where in your body you have stored the hurts and beliefs that are stymieing your full expression now. Accept that those feelings locked in your body so long ago were appropriate when they occurred. Yet, while the feelings may have been relevant then, the interpretation that you made about who you are, and what is possible for your life is most likely not true! Now it is time to identify what you made it mean about you and then to release all those old fears and beliefs. You are ready to release the old hurts and fears and allow that frightened inner child to be taken care of by the adult you. Take time to get acquainted with your young self, integrate your body and mind, your young self and your adult self; love your little kid self. Tell your kid self that he or she is going to be cared for and everything is okay. Indeed, you are good enough right now and you are entitled and capable of fulfilling all your dreams and potential.

2. Trust your inner knowing in order to realize your destiny. We all have an inner wisdom that will guide us toward our life purpose. This is something we can tap to lead us to where we are destined. Listen, pay attention, and allow yourself to drop down into your deeper desires. What is it that you yearn to cocreate with life? It may take some patience and several tries before you can begin to hear it—discerning between your authentic guidance and your mind chatter based upon old beliefs. The outside noise is loud. Know that your best guide is inside you and listen.

3. Develop the power of collaborative relationship with others in order to step into the biggest game possible and begin to participate in changing the world for the better! There is great power in collaborative relationships. Yet, rather than

simply having friends who are supportive, patting us on the back with words of encouragement, Katherine teaches us how to form evolutionary partnerships. These are based on shared vision and bonded by the future we want to create, supportive of each other and encouraging of each other to stand in our power instead of blame and victimhood. When we interact with others in this partnership model, we are building a generative world for ourselves and everyone else.

The meeting of two personalities is like the contact of two chemical substances: if there is any reaction, both are transformed.

—Carl Jung

NURTURING YOUR RELATIONSHIPS

The most nurturing and also the most challenging human connection we have is usually with our significant other—our romantic mate. This relationship has inspired more music, poetry, books, monuments, and heroic deeds than any other relationship in the history of human beings. And it has also caused anger, grief, pain, illnesses, violence, and even death for countless people, too.

In today's busy and fragmented world, can we find our soul mate? Arielle Ford, relationship expert and best-selling author of *The Soulmate Secret*,[9] says yes you can! And there is someone for you regardless of how old you are and what imperfections you think you have. Using her advice, her mother-in-law found her

---

[9] Arielle Ford, *The Soulmate Secret* (New York: Harper Collins, 2011), http://soulmatesecret.com/blog

soul mate at 80 years of age, and they lived happily together until they were parted by death several years later. Arielle found her own soulmate, her husband, Brian, now of 14 years, when she was in her mid-40s.

What, then, is a soulmate? Arielle defines it as someone with whom you can be 100 percent yourself; share unconditional love; someone who, when you look into their eyes, you feel that you are home. This is oftentimes your romantic partner, but he or she can also be your close friend or a family member. Give your loved ones more attention and that energy will bring more of that loving, nurturing frequency into your life. There is someone for you and that person is looking for you, too.

She cites herself as an example of how a good relationship can greatly enhance your life. Before Arielle met her husband, Brian, she was a type A, adrenaline junkie, and a successful author, TV producer, co-founder of Spiritual Cinema Circle, and president of a PR agency representing Deepak Chopra, Jack Canfield, and other experts. She was, as she freely admits, a basket case with too much going on and multitasking herself into a tizzy. Now she is 90 percent mellower; making three times more money; and she feels completely cherished, supported, and adored.

If that sounds like something you want, here's how to get it. First, you have to make some effort to try to find it. I know, you have too much to do, not enough time, and maybe you think that it should just happen if it's right. Arielle counters all that by asking, would you say the same thing if it was a job that you are looking for? Of course not. You'll do the research, polish up your resume, get a haircut and proper clothes for the interviews, and maybe obtain additional training, too. Are you going to just hope that it happens in this the most important aspect of your life?

Arielle just completed a global online training program on manifesting a soul mate; over 70,000 people in 171 countries were involved. She found that 95 percent of single people want to find a soul mate, and a large portion of them worry that they are "too something wrong" (too picky, weird, fat, old, live in a remote location, etc.) to attract one.

She has good news! You can fix the only barrier that is stopping you from connecting with your soulmate—your belief that you can't! Arielle suggests that you do what it takes to shift your belief pattern about your lovability, because yes, you are desirable right now. Seek the support of books, workshops, therapists, coaches, and other trained professionals to help you drop the negative self-talk and appreciate that you are perfect for your soulmate, who is also looking for you. Once you believe you are lovable, you will pay more attention to your love life. Go out and participate in activities you care about, let people know that you are interested in meeting people; in general, act like you are interested in a very important aspect of your life. There are many additional ways to meet your soul mate now; the Internet has made us all easily connectable.

> Age does not protect you from love. But love, to some extent, protects you from age.
>
> —*Anais Nin*

Jeff, an old friend of mine who had been single all his life until he was 64 years old, finally met his soulmate online on a matchmaking site. He lived in Ojai, California, and his now-wife lived in Melbourne, Australia. They are now happily married, spending time in Ecuador, Ojai, and a small town in northeastern Australia. According to Arielle, almost one in five marriages begin online now. The number one way of meeting your soulmate is still through friends, the second is through groups and associations, the third is through work (conferences, clients, etc.), then your neighborhood, and online.

Take heart, you can find and enjoy a fulfilling relationship with your soulmate. Just be open to the quest and follow the wise counsel of these experts who have developed the understanding and experience to find their own soulmates and are now helping numerous others to find theirs. Believe me, my life is much happier, and the challenges are easier to manage with my soulmate in my life. I am grateful to have found mine; and if you are still waiting, may you find yours soon.

How to Nurture Your Relationships

> People take different roads seeking fulfillment and happiness. Just because they're not on your road doesn't mean they've gotten lost.
>
> —*Dalai Lama*

You're in a relationship but you're unhappy, there's conflict, resentment, and unmet expectations, hmm . . . is it better to call it quits and start all over again? Harville Hendrix, PhD, author of several *New York Times* best-selling books on relationships, and featured expert in one of Oprah's top 20 shows, is here to help. Harville is a clinical pastoral counselor (with doctoral degrees from the University of Chicago in both psychology and theology) who is internationally recognized for his work with couples. He and his wife, Helen LaKelly Hunt, PhD, cocreated Imago Relationship Therapy and developed the concept of "conscious partnership."[10]

Harville explains that as much as we may want to escape the pain and frustrations of relationship by isolating or having only

---

[10] www.harvillehendrix.com

short-term or superficial relationships, we crave the deep connection and nurture that a committed long-term relationship, particularly marriage, brings. If we don't fix what is hurting us inside we will continue to bring that into our new relationships. We cannot break free by leaving; we are carrying the culprit inside ourselves. We are born into relationships with our parents, and life is about relationships and relationship is life. So if you want to have a happy life you have to have good relationships. Easier said than done?

Most of us have been there, when we feel despair wondering if we will ever achieve that shiny, happy image that we see in the media—the smiling, loving, and handsome couple, with the healthy, clean-cut, and bright kids, standing in front of their well-kept, paid-off home with an adorable tail-wagging doggy by their side. No wonder we are frustrated and confused! Real life is not static and greeting card perfect, we are dealing with people with different expectations, changing situations, and constant outside pressure every day. But Harville says that like a garden, your relationships can nourish you and keep you healthy and satisfied if you tend them regularly. You can only expect to get a good harvest if you pay attention, water, fertilize, and take out the weeds so that your relationships, like a garden, can grow and flourish. And then the rewards are more than you can ever imagine, they will sustain you and inspire you through the challenges of life.

Harville shared that his insight and wisdom is filtered through scientific research and what he's learned in his relationship with his wife, Helen Hunt, through 35 years of living together.[11] He revealed that early on in his marriage they almost divorced because their lives were so busy that they were not honoring

---

[11] Harville Hendrix, and Helen Hunt, *Receiving Love* (New York: Atria Books, 2004).

what they were teaching. Harville and Helen were both devoting enormous amounts of time to their careers, their nonprofit work, and their combined six children that their personal relationship was neglected and taken for granted. This led to an emotional crisis so severe that they felt that they had only two choices: divorce or truly walk the talk of what they know works—the Conscious Partnership work[12] that they were teaching other couples.

Practicing what they were preaching was not easy. They both came into their relationship with preconceived ideas of how the other should respond, and what different words and actions meant. This is what we frequently do in our relationships, believing that our way of thinking and reacting is natural and obvious—except our partner, who has very different perspectives on what those are, is thinking the same thing! Changing an established relationship is not easy, many habits and patterns have been formed already, and we have to consciously suspend prejudgment to genuinely hear what is being expressed. Harville and Helen had to commit to zero negativity in all communications. This meant there is no negating of the other person, in what they do, say, or who they are—no eye rolling, put-downs, or other unsupportive behavior. Only active, compassionate listening was allowed. This is what they know is needed to build a foundation of trust and respect for each other. For the first three months of their last try for their relationship, there was very little conversation between them—breaking the habits of the "already heard" attitude and subtle and not so hidden put-downs was very hard.

Harville's analogy in shifting a toxic and negative relationship into a healthy and loving one, is that it is like clearing a

---

[12] Harville Hendrix, Couplehood Programs, www.harvillehendrix.com/aboutCASP.html

smoke-filled room. It is only when you start clearing the smoke out do you realize how thick and pervasive it was. Yet they persisted with their commitment to change and gradually they realized how ambivalent they had been about truly being in the marriage. It was only when they agreed to drop the mixed feelings and make an unconditional commitment to each other did they start experiencing the deeply felt connection, the stable and joyful aliveness, and the plateau of joy and happiness that they knew was the definition of a real partnership.

Their children's visits became more fun, and they visited more often, and even the ones who communicated remotely could sense that things were dramatically changed for the good. Each day was more joyful as they continued to reaffirm their commitment to keep their relationship a priority in their lives.

WABI-SABI LOVE

Arielle Ford has a term for this loving of each other while still acknowledging the imperfections in the other, in fact, loving another *because* of his or her quirks! She uses the Japanese concept, *wabi-sabi*,[13] which means appreciating and, in fact, treasuring the very out of the ordinary aspect of an object, person, or nature. An example would be to showcase the crack that occurred in the firing of a hand-sculpted vase or the knots in an old bonsai. It is seeing the unique beauty in the flaws and inconsistencies in our partner and ourselves. People generally just want to be loved for who they are—men want to be respected, appreciated, and listened to, and women want to be cherished, adored, and listened to. To know that your partner

---

[13] Arielle Ford's work, Wabi-Sabi Love, www.wabisabilove.com

knows that you are not perfect and loves you with your idiosyncrasies intact is a very comforting and freeing gift— and one that brings you both closer.

Making your relationship a priority is not just about how many hours you spend on it, it is about the sense of security that you offer each other. The removal of the possibility of negative feedback changes your mind-set and positively affects all aspects of your life and relationship. There is now a solid base to build your relationship and life upon; no hidden landmines are lurking ready to sabotage your stability.

Harville attributes the breakdown of marriage and long-term relationships to "selfness." He says that the growing focus on the self has resulted in a myopic view of life; there is less attention on the relationship and more on oneself. He calls it a culture of narcissism, where we forget that the most nurturing relationship we can have is when we are fully engaged with another. Oftentimes, we only want to escape or avoid the pain that occurs when there are unmet expectations and misunder- standings. We bolt out of the relationship instead of looking inward to see that we are actually a good part of the problem. The more we focus on self-preservation and do not recognize that we also need to change and make a commitment to the relationship, the more pain we will have. As long as we keep concentrating on keeping ourselves exactly as we are and expecting the other to change, we will experience the same lack of long-term connection and love with either the same person or a series of people. Instead, look and tend the garden of your relationship together so that you may both enjoy the bountiful, luscious, and nurturing produce you are cultivating.

> Not everything that is faced can be changed. But nothing can
> be changed until it is faced.
>
> —*James Baldwin*

UNCOUPLING

But what if you have done all the things that Harville recommended and are still prepared to release the relationship? We are living longer in an increasingly complex world, which is changing at a faster rate than all the generations before us experienced. It is possible that you may have completed your current relationship with your partner. Katherine Woodward Thomas wrote about the dissolution of her own marriage in her best-selling book, *Calling in "The One,"* in her new course called Conscious Uncoupling.[14] Katherine was initially terrified of the concept of uncoupling from her husband who led her to write *Calling in "The One"* many years ago. She was worried that people would judge her and invalidate her work, and what she would do now at 53 years old and a single mom?

Being a practicing clinical psychotherapist, she delved into her own healing and analysis of the lessons to be learned. She found that it is possible to have conscious uncoupling. Her separation from her husband and former life was done with love and consideration for each other and their beloved daughter. There were no recriminations or blame, and together they committed to the loving completion of their relationship and healing the scars left from previous breakups. The unconditional love that she and her ex-husband shared is intact. Their relationship as a couple was complete, but they could still care for each other and share in the nurture and well-being of their daughter.

Katherine found that you could use the catalyst of the major life change of divorce to heal old wounds. She, her ex-husband, and their daughter are now what Katherine calls an "expanded

---

[14] http://evolvingwisdom.com/consciousuncoupling/free-online-class/

family," with their new loves adding to the relationship instead of being divisive forces. She offers a free online course for people who have come to this stage of their relationship.[15]

There is hope and love in knowing that when you are clear in your life purpose that even in the midst of one of the most painful and disrupting events in your life, you can learn, grow, and heal from it. You gain the lessons and clarify your vision of what and how you are to fully live and contribute in the world.

> Problems in relationship occur because each person is concentrating on what is missing in the other person.
>
> —*Wayne Dyer*

FURTHER THOUGHTS ON RELATIONSHIPS

People not in deep relationships are casualties of our culture, said Harville Hendrix; people have to be engaged with others to thrive and be happy. Reach out to connect with friends, join social interest groups, find simpatico social contacts, and work consciously to build a community around you that supports one another. To further reinforce how important meaningful relationships are, Harville cites statistics that show people without one have life spans that are 8 to 10 years shorter, higher rates of illness, and more medical complaints. Feeling alone activates anxiety, and depression rates are enormously higher among lonely people.

---

[15] http://evolvingwisdom.com/consciousuncoupling/free-online-class/
www.ArtOfConsciousCompletion.com

Another caution Harville pointed out is that we too often reach for the quick fix, which is usually not the long-term solution. A good example of this is the large number of pharmaceutical drugs prescribed today that are masking people's anxiety and other negative emotions rather than resolving them. People are not fundamentally helped, but they are numbed to their emotional pain, which results in decreased vitality, lowered sexual drive, and a decreased interest in social activities and life in general. These mood-altering drugs may be useful for a temporary crisis but they are not to be used on a long-term basis, because you have to deal with the issues to make real change and over time you can become habituated to the drugs. There are many reasons to take steps to seek the support you need to shift your inner landscape so that you are more at peace with yourself.

Isolation and aloneness are detrimental to all aspects of human wellness. Harville encourages us to participate in social and community groups, even when we have a life partner. We need the social and mental stimulation, satisfaction, and the support that come from being in and contributing to community.

Like most everyone today, I have very heavy demands on my time, but I choose to make time for close friends who nourish me. The solution to the shortage of time is to find friends who share similar interests with you and whose time schedule is similarly challenged. One of my good friends is Jan. She is the head parish nurse for the area's hospital group, and she is also a medical pre-surgery hypnotist, professional singer, videographer, and humanitarian; on top of that she is happily married and has an organic garden. As she describes our relationship— it's high quality and low maintenance.

Develop relationships with people who share your vision for life and establish the comfort and agreement that you will be available for each other whenever needed but with no guilt trip about any obligatory connections. You get together when you both find time, share a common interest, or when one of you needs a boost. It's a great way of maintaining a needed source of support while honoring the busyness of your lives.

The success of religious organizations and community organizations is in large part due to their small groups (choirs, soup kitchen workers, volunteer committees, etc.) where people can come together to build strong and supportive relationships while offering help for others. It is what keeps the organizations and its members alive and the community thriving. Our species developed through the support of relationships, and this is how we can continue to thrive. Indeed, the saying "no man is an island" is even truer today since we have scientific proof of our need for social connection. Take courage; see the other person not as an extension of yourself but as a separate and amazing being who is in your life. You will be happy and flourish in that warm, trusting, and respectful community that you can build around yourself.

> We can only be said to be alive in those moments when our hearts are conscious of our treasures.
>
> —*Thornton Wilder*

GRATITUDE

I'm grateful you are in my community, and I hope that in some small way I am contributing to yours. Giving gratitude is a sure way of feeling happier, it reminds us of the positives instead of dwelling on what we consider miserable in our lives. A 10-week study done by researchers at the University of California at Davis and University of Miami showed that people who were asked to list five things daily that they were grateful for were 25 percent happier with their lives, had fewer health issues, and exercised 1.5 hours per week more than the control group, who listed five things that bothered them daily. They were also more optimistic about their futures.[16]

The thoughts we think trigger physiological changes, which impact our mental and physical health. This biofeedback system is powerful and is the basis of the field of psychoneuro-immunology that is proving we are, indeed, what we think. There is a complex relationship between thoughts, moods, brain chemistry, endocrine function, and functioning of other physiological systems in our bodies. Increase your positive thoughts, like gratitude, and you increase your emotional well-being and your physical health, too. Gratitude is powerful and it makes you happier!

> Scared and sacred are spelled with the same letters. Awful proceeds from the same root word as awesome. Terrify and terrific.
>
> Every negative experience holds the seed of transformation.
> —*Alan Cohen*

---

[16] Robert A. Emmons, PhD, and Mike McCullough, PhD, study on gratitude, 2011, http://greatergood.berkeley.edu/article/item/pay_it_forward; and *The Psychology of Gratitude*, 1st ed., Robert A. Emmons Michael E, McCullough (New York: Oxford University Press, 2004).

7

SPIRIT

There is a light in this world, a healing spirit more powerful than any darkness we may encounter. We sometimes lose sight of this force when there is suffering, too much pain. Then suddenly, the spirit will emerge through the lives of ordinary people who hear a call and answer in extraordinary ways.

—*Mother Teresa*

There is a Chinese saying, "when you're in extreme danger, wrap your arms around Buddha's feet." It is the Chinese version of "there are no atheists in foxholes." The general meaning is the same; when people feel acutely threatened or are in dire straits, they hope or believe in a higher power to pull them through what they don't think they can do by themselves.

People refer to what sustains and supports them by many names: God, Spirit, Jesus, Allah, Buddha, Mohammed, Krishna, Greater Power, Nature, and many more. Most believe that there is a power, a source of ultimate energy. This is what has kept people going through times of immense stress, provided inner counsel in times of confusion, and given more meaning to joyous events. How do we regard this core belief and what can we learn from people who have devoted their lives to honor it? There are common themes throughout the major spiritual traditions, which I will share here. Please interpret and use them as it resonates with your individual belief system. In this chapter I will refer to this greater power as "Spirit." Please substitute the name that is meaningful for you.

THE FELT SENSE

The Rev. Cynthia Bourgeault, PhD, is an Episcopal priest, internationally known teacher, retreat and conference leader, and principal teacher and adviser for The Contemplative

Society.[1] She is the author of seven books, including *The Wisdom Jesus, The Meaning of Mary Magdalene*, and *Centering Prayer and Inner Awakening*.[2] Rev. Bourgeault is emphatic in saying don't *believe* in a greater power, *feel* it empirically in your heart. Understand the heart as the ancient traditions knew and taught it: as an organ of spiritual perception. We need to shift from the thinking mode into experiencing with our hearts and feelings. In that level of perception, we truly know the power and love of Spirit and in knowing we are fortified and the eye of our heart is opened.[3]

She cites His Holiness the Dalai Lama's important teaching: "Believe nothing, no matter where you read it, or who said it, no matter if I have said it, unless it agrees with your own reason and your own common sense," as an example that this concept of personal verification is a common teaching among religions. So how does one get to know Spirit? And why?

> The spiritual force transcends all. I feel this great creative and spiritual force within me that is greater than faith, greater than ambition, greater than confidence, greater than determination, greater than vision. It is all these combined. My brain becomes magnetized with this dominating force, which I hold in my hand.
>
> —*Bruce Lee*

The power of Spirit kept me alive. As a child, the arbitrary and explosive abuse I received was frightening and acutely painful. Even more than the physical pain, it was the inexplicable and unpredictable nature of the assaults that

---

[1] www.contemplative.org

[2] www.contemplative.org/cynthia.html

[3] Cynthia Bourgeault, *The Wisdom Way of Knowing* (San Francisco, CA: Jossey-Bass, 2003).

hurt so deeply. I climbed trees to hide so I could reduce the probability of being maltreated. There, in the arms of nature, I spent many a soothing hour, just being. In that space and openness, I felt the presence of Spirit. It was soft and powerful, gentle and strong; I felt at home and protected.

Gradually, I learned how to call on that power even in the midst of yet another beating. Spirit inside me kept me from losing my mind trying to figure out why. I knew instinctively that I was going to be okay even when all physical evidence was telling me that I was most probably going to die at any moment. My life is blessed because in the fear and pain, I found something much more meaningful and powerful, which has guided and fortified me in all my endeavors in life.

With Spirit in your life, you get to live in the glorious, multilayer reality with a sense of wonder and joy instead of in the miserable dumbing down of life without Spirit. Ah, the happiness of seeing the kaleidoscope colors of our existence instead of focusing on the minutiae. When we live without a higher purpose and belief, life can seem rather mundane and without deep meaning.

Viktor Frankl, a psychiatrist, Holocaust survivor, and the author of the global best seller, *Man's Search for Meaning* states it eloquently:

> The truth—that love is the ultimate and the highest goal to which man can aspire. Then I grasped the meaning of the greatest secret that human poetry and human thought and belief have to impart: *The salvation of man is through love and in love.* I understood how a man who has nothing left in this world still may know bliss, be it only for a brief moment, in the contemplation of his beloved. In a position of utter desolation, when man cannot express himself in positive action, when his only achievement may consist in enduring

his sufferings in the right way—an honorable way—in such a position man can, through loving contemplation of the image he carries of his beloved, achieve fulfillment. For the first time in my life I was able to understand the meaning of the words, *"The angels are lost in perpetual contemplation of an infinite glory."* [my italics][4]

Here was a man who had suffered through the worst imaginable experiences in the Nazi concentration camps and lost all but one of his extended family there, and yet he speaks of marveling at angels and the infinite glory. Wow, that is powerful.

How do we access that infinite love in our hearts so that we are living fully and consciously? Rev. Bourgeault says as a Christian minister she learned the access point through centering prayer, "a no-frills form of meditation in the Christian tradition," popularized by her teacher, Fr. Thomas Keating. She encourages you to start from wherever you are currently in the practice of meditation. In Chapter 3, Life Purpose—Yours, there is information on one way of meditating; you can find many more in books, courses and workshops from various traditions, online, and in your spiritual community. You can only run a marathon after you've been practicing for a while; be patient with yourself, as you meditate your field of perception will gradually broaden. Even with the slightest effort you can begin to change your life; it's all incremental and rewarding.

With meditation you will gain much greater emotional flexibility, not take the "I" so seriously, and develop more resilience, and become less judgmental. A sense of coherence will gradually emerge, and you will feel an inner calmness as you undergo and experience the neurological rewiring, which

---

[4] Viktor Frankl, *Man's Search for Meaning* (New York: Pocket Books, 1997).

enables you to live a unitive reality on an ongoing basis. Your capacity to deal with what is happening will expand, and you will not be easily rattled, instead you will live from a grounding in equanimity.

If this sounds like the way you want to live life, practice centering prayer and meditation, and you will feel and know that greater power of Spirit, which sustains you. Again, know that however and whatever you do to start is good, all ways lead to more peace and happiness. One small note, for people who have a high level of inner chatter, you may find that during the first few times you meditate, your inner critic will come up. Acknowledge that judging voice and put it aside, you are making progress.

> You do not need to work to become spiritual. You are spiritual; you need only to remember that fact. Spirit is within you. God is within you.
> —*Julia Cameron,* God Is No Laughing Matter

THE THREE PILLARS OF CHINESE WISDOM

Master Chungliang Al Huang grew up in the violent turmoil and uncertainty of China's Nationalist-Communist Civil War. In that fierce mayhem and hostilities he learned that each day was a gift. Along with that felt sense of Spirit, he also was immersed in the traditional study of Tai Ji, Kung Fu, brush calligraphy, and the classic Chinese scholarly arts from a young age. He studied the three pillars of Chinese wisdom—Taoism, Confucianism, and Buddhism—which furthered his ability to greet the precariousness of war with equanimity. He absorbed the philosophies of the three pillars, the power of nature in the Tao, proper interpersonal relationships from Confucian teaching, and the eternity of life in Buddhism. He learned how to be happy in the moment. Master Huang has made it his life's work to teach these lessons globally and to write about them in his many books.[5]

Master Huang is a philosopher, taijiquan (Tai Ji) master, and copresenter with many world leaders including the Dalai Lama, of religion and spiritual philosophy. He is the founder and president of the Living Tao Foundation based in the United States, and the International Lan Ting Institute, located in the sacred mountains of China. He was featured in the inaugural program of Bill Moyers' renowned PBS series, *A World of Ideas*, and has many close alliances with other philosophers including Alan Watts, Joseph Campbell, Houston Smith, Joseph Needham, Gregory Bateson, and John Blofeld.

How, then, does one attain happiness and connection to Spirit? Master Huang says that first you have to know yourself. Learn and listen to yourself to develop the "Doctrine of the Mean,"[6] the "unwobbling pivot" as Ezra Pound translates it.[7] You have to be like clay as it is being molded on a potter's wheel: flexible, rising, and centered amidst the fast-turning spin. You are always "getting there," because when you get there, you are here, so by definition you are never there. Be centered in the chaos, in that unwobbling pivot is happiness.

---

[5] Chungliang Al Huang, *Embrace Tiger, Return to Mountain: The Essence of Tai Ji* (Philadelphia: Singing Dragon, 2011); *Thinking Body, Dancing Mind: Taosports for Extraordinary Performance in Athletics, Business, and Life* (New York: Bantam, 1994); and *Quantum Soup: Fortune Cookies in Crisis* (Philadelphia: Singing Dragon, 2011).

[6] (Chinese: 中庸; pinyin: zhōng yōng).

[7] Ezra Pound, *Confucius* (New York: New Directions Publishing Corporation, 1969).

Master Chungliang Al Huang, a philosopher, taijiquan
(Tai Ji) master, and copresenter with many world leaders
including the Dalai Lama, of religion and spiritual
philosophy. He is the founder and president of the Living
Tao Foundation based in the United States, and the
International Lan Ting Institute in China. For more photos
and information of all the experts in the book, please go to
www.MarilynTam.com

Instead of looking at happiness as being a constant state,
regard the polarities as part of the whole or holistic coherence.
"The Great Way" is not difficult for those who are not
attached to preferences.[8] Happiness is not the elimination
of all your negatives and accentuating of the positives, said
Master Huang, because then you will be only one-dimensional.
In the Chinese yin-yang symbol, each side flows into the
other; there is no beginning and no end, and together they
make up the whole (see Figure 7.1). Without spring there is no
summer, without summer then no fall, and with no fall there is
no winter.

---

[8] Seng-ts'an, Third Chinese Patriarch: *Hsin-Hsin Ming: Verses on the Faith-Mind.*

Figure 7.1   Yin-Yang symbol.

We need the entire range of emotions to fully feel and live; embrace your fear and watch its metamorphosis into understanding and then into release and joy. This is the teaching of Tao Te Ching (I Ching), Verse 25:[9]

Something mysteriously formed,
Born before Heaven and Earth.
In the silence and the void,
Standing alone and unchanging,
Ever present and in motion.
Perhaps it is the mother of ten thousand things.
I do not know its name
Call it Tao. For lack of a better word, I call it great.
Being great, it flows
It flows far away.
Having gone far, it returns.
Therefore, "Tao is great;
Heaven is great;
Earth is great;
The king is also great."
These are the four great powers of the universe,

---

[9] Lao Tzu, *Tao Te Ching* (New York: Vintage, 1997).

And the king is one of them.
Man follows Earth.
Earth follows Heaven.
Heaven follows the Tao.
Tao follows what is natural.

Get out of the little me self into the bigger self, like a dew drop as it merges into the shiny sea, you will realize the power and magic in the unity of all that is. There is only now, the present moment. If you are not feeling happy now, know that you have the option to change; happiness is intrinsic in us, and it is a choice. You are not a human doing, you are a human being, and you can choose how to *be*.

Buddhist teaching is that life, death, and renewal is a cycle. We come from somewhere, we are here now, and then we depart for somewhere else. Do not attach to things; we may die tonight and wake up to a new life. In living that way we are present to what is here now, and we can choose to be content with what is; in that contentment we are happy. So live your life purpose because when you are living with meaning and purpose you are truly alive and then naturally you will be happy.

The first peace, which is the most important, is that which comes within the souls of people when they realize their relationship, their oneness with the universe and all its powers, and when they realize at the center of the universe dwells the Great Spirit, and that its center is really everywhere, it is within each of us.

—*Black Elk*

Spiritual Awakening

Joan Borysenko had her spiritual awakening experience at age 10. It came about from what was a very difficult situation. In Chapter 3, Life Purpose – Yours, Joan shared the story of a phobia she developed in which her entire family would be killed by any one of the fearsome jungle creatures in the horror movie her parents took her to see when she was 10 years old. Neither the therapist that her parents sought out to help her nor all they tried to do themselves alleviated her neurosis. Her obsessive fear persisted until, in a moment of inspired panic, Joan began a series of deep and intense prayers and meditation where she finally found relief and resolution. From then on Joan knew that the power of Spirit was real and present in her life. Even though it is unseen, this extraordinary sense of love, power, and guidance is available for anyone to connect to at any time. Human beings, according to Joan, have a built-in guidance system that takes us to the source of being. We're hardwired for Spirit. But rather than being embedded in our brain, the magnet for our spiritual journey is located in the heart.

Joan has written many books[10] and facilitated lectures and workshops that blend science, psychology, and spirituality in a unique and powerful way. She has witnessed how Spirit has given support and hope to people going through distressing times. Connecting to Spirit gives us the resilience to handle tough times, and that is also when it may be more

---

[10] Joan Borysenko, *Fire in the Soul: A New Psychology of Spiritual Optimism* (New York: Grand Central Publishing, 1994); *The Ways of The Mystic: Seven Paths to God* (Carlsbad, CA: Hay House, 1997); *Pocketful of Miracles: Prayer, Meditations, and Affirmations to Nurture Your Spirit Every Day of the Year* (New York: Grand Central Publishing, 1994); and *Your Soul's Compass— What Is Spiritual Guidance?* (Carlsbad, CA: Hay House, 2007).

challenging to keep the connection. However, the people who manage to hold on to the paradox are the ones who survive and thrive.

Jim Collins, in his book, *Good to Great*,[11] coined what he called the "Stockdale Syndrome." Jim Stockdale was an American prisoner of war in Vietnam for seven-and-a-half years. He attributed his survival and ability to rebound and advance in his career to vice admiral after his release to his faith that success is possible and in fact inevitable, while realistically confronting the dreadful facts of the present circumstances. He also said that the ones who wore rose colored glasses and denied that they were in a dire situation were the first to die in the POW camps. It was the ability to hold the paradox that yes, the current situation is unpalatable and still work with everything you have to achieve what you envision that allowed others to survive. Faith in Spirit will support you in that journey.

Joan believes that the Spirit has consciousness and compassion, and it is always changing and evolving. And because we are part of that energy, we can also evolve and have compassion—we are made in that image, which is infinitely creative and full of possibilities. With that we have meaning in life and are stress hardy.

How does one access that power? Each has his/her own ways of tapping into the source. Joan's advice is to find the doorway that works for you; you will know when it is right. The biggest entries globally are via nature, music, and meditation. Remember that all things will pass, either good or bad. Fully feel your feelings, you will not drown in them but instead the feelings will lift if you allow them to be. Rather than denying the grief, feel the grief and eventually it will lessen. Find solace and support in music, poetry, nature, and

---

[11] Jim Collins, *Good to Great* (New York: Harper Business, 2001).

in people who have endured similar pain and have become wiser from the experience.

Call on the power of Spirit and you will feel relief.[12] Joan shares an old Yiddish folk tale about King Solomon's ring. Inside the band was inscribed, "GAM ZU YAAVOR" (this, too, shall pass). It is a good reminder for us to be grateful for the moment—whatever it may have in store for indeed, this, too, shall pass.

> Take the first step in faith. You don't have to see the whole staircase, just take the first step.
>
> —*Martin Luther King Jr.*

---

[12] Joan Borysenko, *Fire in the Soul: A New Psychology of Spiritual Optimism* (New York: Grand Central Publishing, 1994).

8

YOUR BODY

No medicine cures what happiness cannot.
> —*Gabriel García Márquez*

F ifty-eight percent of Americans have postponed, cut
back, or skipped seeking medical care reportedly because
of cost in 2012.[1] In 2009, the latest available comparison by
country survey done by Commonwealth Fund, 43 percent of
American women between age 19 and 64 reduced or skipped
medical care for this reason; the highest in the 11 countries
studied.[2] Experts cite the relatively high price of U.S. health
care as the reason that Americans don't seek professional
medical care more often. I wonder if the common feelings
of not having enough time and the American attitudes of
"grit it out" and "it's nothing, really" factor into Americans'
reluctance to seek medical care. I know that I have rationalized
not seeking medical care based on some of the above reasons in
addition to the usual cost factor, and the same was true for
many of the clients who came to the health care clinic where
I was a partner.

Health is often defined as the absence of illness, injury, and
disease. Actually, there is a wide spectrum of health—from
being vibrantly alive and vigorous to being at death's door.[3] We
are, in large part, in control of how vibrantly healthy we are by
how we choose to think, eat, and live each day. When we are out

---

[1] Kaiser Family Foundation, "Kaiser Public Opinion, Health Security
Watch" (June 2012). www.kff.org/healthpollreport/CurrentEdition/security/
upload/8322.pdf

[2] Commonwealth Fund, "Realizing Health Reform's Potential." http://www
.commonwealthfund.org/~/media/Files/Publications/Issue%20Brief/2012/
Jul/1606_Robertson_oceans_apart_reform_brief.pdf

[3] Please note that the scope of this book can only address the range of health
separate from critical illnesses, which would require much deeper discourse
than possible in this chapter.

of balance, we are susceptible to a range of illnesses and we age much faster, too!

> While situations, encounters or events may seem intrinsically "stressful," it is truly how an individual perceives and reacts to an event that determines whether or not the stress response is activated.
>
> —*Institute of HeartMath*

MOODS, STRESS, AND HEALTH

Stress is the biggest cause of illness today. Your body responds to stress the same way our ancestors reacted to being chased by a predator; your body releases the flight or fight hormones, adrenaline or noradrenaline and cortisol, which gets the body ready to respond to physical danger. During stressful periods, our immune system, digestive, and reproductive functions are repressed so that the body can deal with the immediate danger. But over time, with high and frequent stress, our body functions are weakened, and we become vulnerable to viruses, bacteria, and other environmental toxins as well as the breakdown of our bodily systems.

Janet Hranicky, PhD, founder and president of The American Health Institute,[4] specializing in customized antiaging programs and natural medical products, confirms the powerful connection between health and our mental attitude. Janet was also a long-time collaborator and associate of Dr. Carl Simonton, the pioneering radiologist and oncologist in the mind-body connection (psychoneuroimmunology) in fighting cancer. Janet

---

[4] Janet Hranicky, PhD, www.ahealth.com

has deep experience in what happens when the body's cells go rogue, which is what happens with cancer cells. She explained that stress and unhappiness are big factors in weakening the body, accelerating aging and disease.

Janet cites their work at Simonton Cancer Center where they counseled stage-four cancer patients on how to shift their emotional stage to a happier one and doubled their median survival time. Good health starts with a favorable mind-set—surround yourself with people and things that bring you joy and spend time in nature and move away from things that do the reverse. Her recommendation is supported by her own work and other research.[5]

Marc Berman's PhD research showed that being in nature, and even looking at pictures of nature can alleviate depression and improve memory and cognitive functioning in both the average person as well as the clinically depressed.[6] The most fascinating information to me was that you don't even have to particularly enjoy your time in nature; the test subjects were walking in a cold arboretum in the Michigan winter! Other test subjects who spent the same amount of time, an hour walking in a busy traffic urban setting, did not achieve the same mood and cognitive improvement. Our brains can rest and replenish our working memory and attention systems in the peaceful state of nature. Spending time in nature is powerful and nurturing.

Janet explains that you have a choice in how you greet each day. Smile as soon as you wake up, take a few deep breaths upon waking, and set the tone for the day that way. She is so

---

[5] www.researchmatters.ku.edu/2009/march/happy.shtml This correlation between health and happiness is verified in 140 countries by joint research from Kansas University and Gallup Poll.

[6] Marc Berman, "A Walk in the Park Gives Mental Boost to People with Depression," *Science Daily*, May 14, 2012, www.sciencedaily.com/releases/2012/05/120514134303.htm

enthusiastic about her work and life that I am smiling as I write; her positive energy is so infectious!

Which is another point—your mood can influence people around you and you can choose how you want people to behave toward you just by your attitude. Sigal G. Barsade, PhD, showed that by adding a person with an assigned emotion to a group, she could guide the group's mood and performance— all without the group's conscious awareness. When the planted person was enthusiastic and engaged, the entire group per-formed better and was more collaborative, and the converse was true when the planted person was withdrawn and uninterested.[7] This is powerful information to have as you conduct yourself in business and life—know that your frame of mind can help or hinder you.

> Tension is who you think you should be. Relaxation is who you are.
>
> —*Chinese proverb*

Janet describes the underlying science behind health and longevity; it's all quantum integrative biophysics. Physical health is the downstream of your upstream emotional and spiritual health. The invisible energy patterns in the bio-energy field of the body is the focus of the field of epigenetics, the science that studies people's emotional states and how people's interaction with their environment impacts the gene expression and the manifestation of healthy or unhealthy cells. Your psychic energy and emotional state is transmitted into every cellular communication in your body and in how your DNA is

---

[7] Sigal G. Barsade, "The Ripple Effect: Emotional Contagion and Its Influence on Group Behavior," http://asq.sagepub.com/content/47/4/644.abstract

triggered to express into your physical body. Janet is engaged in this leading-edge work, and she encourages us to mentally take regular snapshots of our moods and know that we can change our energetics right now. You have a choice of how to direct your focus and influence the foundation of your emotional states, beliefs, and physical health.

Having worked for over 30 years with cancer patients, Janet explained the direct correlation between the current interest in antiaging/longevity medicine and cancer medicine. Both are based on dealing with how to make the cells operate optimally.[8] Aging and cancer happen when the cells develop errors in duplication and, in time, with sufficient numbers of incorrect cell reproduction, results in malfunction or aging in the body. Our stressful emotional states of anger, fear, and pain over time damage our cell expression, whereas faith, happiness, and peaceful feelings help sustain and improve the potential for healthy development of our cells. Asking yourself, "is this worth getting sick and dying over?" will give you another perspective on the issue you are stressed about. Know that your self-talk can enhance or diminish your life and well-being. Now it is proven scientifically what so many spiritual teachers from different religions have been saying: you can heal your body by thinking positive thoughts. What an exciting time to be living!

> A happy person is not a person in a certain set of circum-
> stances, but rather a person with a certain set of attitudes.
> —*Hugh Downs*

Janet shared other things we can do to enhance and improve our health. Start each day with an alkaline base—drink a tablespoon of lemon juice in a glass of water, juice fresh green

---

[8] http://drhranicky.com

vegetables, make a green smoothie or purchase green drinks (choose ones with less sugar) to give your body the proper alkaline base. Eat live food; eat food as close to the source and nature as possible, including raw foods like fresh salads, vegetables, nuts, and fruits. Keep your metabolic processes functioning well by taking supplemental nutraceuticals[9] that can help the body eliminate toxins and supply needed nutrients for the body's metabolic processes to function properly. Drink lots of clean, filtered water. Move toward work/life balance. In what you eat, drink, and do, are you overscheduling and overcommitting to things? Moderation is the key. Be aware that we are interrelated and the planet impacts us as well as vice versa.

DIET, EXERCISE, MIND, AND HEALTH

If we could give every individual the right amount of nourishment and exercise, not too little and not too much, we would have found the safest way to health.

—Hippocrates

This reminder for us to live in balance is very important, as Joan Borysenko, PhD, a pioneer in psychoneuroimmunology (mind-body medicine), can attest. Joan co-founded one of the first mind-body clinics in the world and taught the science at Harvard Medical School and Tufts Medical School. She truly understands the power of the mind to influence the well-being

---

[9] Nutraceuticals are products extracted or condensed from foods that provide health benefits; for example, milk thistle, an herb known to help cleanse the liver, is available as a herbal tea; tomatoes and carrots have beta carotene and lycopene, which are available as dietary supplements; and cold-water fish and krill supply omega 3, which is available in capsule form.

of the body; her book, *Minding the Body, Mending the Mind*[10] has sold several hundred thousand copies globally.

As a young researcher in the 1970s, Joan read *Diet for a Small Planet* by Frances Lappe and overnight became a strict vegetarian, making her own bread, growing her own vegetable garden, foraging for wild plants, and eating only organic foods. However, in her earnest commitment to reduce her impact on the planet, she was ignoring what it was actually doing to her body. She lost a lot of weight and was down to a sickly 97 pounds, had no energy, and a pallid complexion. Then the rumor started that she, a cancer researcher, was dying of leukemia.

She was prompted to reexamine her lifestyle and to see if she was actually healthy and living as an example of the conscious healthy life she was espousing. She knew that health and spirituality are about awareness, and she had to admit that her diet was not suitable for her. Her body needed more nutrients than what she was getting in her strict vegetarian diet.[11] She investigated what an optimal diet would be for her and added small amounts of fish and chicken to her food and slowly regained a healthy amount of weight. In all matters, we have to analyze and determine what is appropriate for us instead of blindly accepting what people tell us is good for us.

Joan shared her definition of health derived from what she learned from her own experience and her professional research: When you are healthy, you have excellent energy, feel good, and can move well based on your age and physical conditions. People in wheelchairs can be healthy with the limited range of

---

[10] Joan Borysenko, *Minding the Mind, Mending the Body*, rev. ed. (Cambridge, MA: Da Capo Press, 2007).

[11] In the 1970s, the science was still very young in food nutrients analysis and what the body needs to maintain optimal health. Joan was not getting enough protein and other nutrients from her diet.

motion that is possible for them. She spoke about her work with patients with multiple sclerosis, including Jimmy Huger, a former Olympian. You can, like him, choose to be your healthiest self regardless of your current physical condition.

Health is more than an absence of disease; there is a wide range to good health—from just not being sick to feeling vitally alive. Joan cites Dr. Claude Bernard's definition of homeostasis as health: health is when all the systems of the body are working together to the best effect.[12]

Diet and exercise are important to maintaining good health. Before you embark on any significant changes to your current lifestyle of diet and exercise, it is vital that you establish some base markers of your health conditions so that you are assured that the changes are advisable and within your current physical capabilities. Diving into an overly ambitious program of diet and exercise without knowing what is going on in your body could be injurious. Consult medical practitioners who are up-to-date with the latest research to learn if you have any preexisting conditions or borderline health issues that need to be considered in conjunction with your new health plan. Some common things to check for include, but are not limited to, prediabetic and diabetic conditions, any cardiopulmonary weaknesses, your inflammatory markers like C-reactive protein, and TSH, T3, and T4 levels for thyroid. After you have obtained information about your body, then you can safely and properly design your optimal health program.

Once you establish a diet and exercise plan that works for you, stay with it and regularly monitor it to check for improvements and modifications; your body and mind will both thank you.

---

[12] Claude Bernard, MD, the pioneer in modern experimental physiology, www.cerebromente.org.br/n06/historia/bernard_i.htm

Since I travel globally for speaking and consulting engagements, there are many times when it would be easy to skip eating well and neglect exercising "just this one time." When I've succumbed to taking the easy way out, I've paid for it in how I feel physically and in my mental clarity. When I don't adhere to my eating, exercise, and meditation practices, I feel sluggish, mentally foggy, and jet lagged.

Of course we have to be flexible and adjust to the environment we are in. I may get my exercise by walking around airports instead of hiking, walking, swimming, doing tai chi, or jumping on my rebounder, but the key is that I'm getting some kind of workout. Choose the forms of exercise that you like; no matter how good the exercise, it is only effective if you do it regularly. Vary your exercise routine so that you stay interested and motivated. Do a combination of cardio, strength building, and stretching exercises. You are more likely to continue if you like the program as compared to doing it only because it is good for you. Walking is an easy way to get some exercise, and it takes no equipment and you can do it almost anywhere.

"Physical activity is the wonder drug," Centers for Disease Control and Prevention Director Dr. Thomas R. Frieden told reporters. "It makes you healthier and happier. More Americans are making a great first step in getting more physical activity."[13] The good news is that any small increase in physical activity is better than none, and once you start there is more probability that you will continue and eventually do more.

Joan Borysenko speaks from her clinical and personal experience on the power of exercise to improve one's mood—30 minutes a day, five days a week will increase your cardio health and overall well-being. She also cites the

---

[13] August 7, 2012, statement released with The Centers for Disease Control and Prevention 2010 study of 23,129 adults on exercise and health.

many studies, that show owning a pet (dogs in particular) is good for one's health. Walking your dog daily becomes a way to ensure that you are also getting exercise. The companionship of a pet has been shown to enhance and improve the quality and longevity of life. National Institutes of Health research[14] has shown that people with pets are healthier, live longer, are less stressed, and recover from stress easier and quicker than people with no pets. Of course, your lifestyle may not be suitable for you to have a pet. Pets take regular care, and it would be a disservice to yourself and your pet if you adopted a pet when you already have too much to manage. The underlying message is that when you interact with others, including a pet, in a loving way and feel loved back, coupled with regular exercise, you'll be healthier, live longer, be happier and less stressed, too.

> As I see it, every day you do one of two things: build heath or produce disease in yourself.
>
> —*Adelle Davis*

Joan shared another good reason to minimize stress—stress makes you fat in the most harmful way. When the body is under stress, the hormone cortisol is released and belly fat increases with the amount of cortisol in the body. Belly fat is the most dangerous kind of fat in the body; it is linked to diabetes, heart disease, and premature death.[15] Today, 90 percent of patient visits to primary care doctors are for stress-related illnesses. Needless to say, this is a good reminder for us to do all that we can to keep our stress levels low; the consequences of high stress are alarming. Exercise is a great way to keep our stress level in a

---

[14] "Can Pets Help Keep You Healthy?" *NIH News in Health*, http://newsinhealth.nih.gov/2009/February/feature1.htm

[15] www.webmd.com/diet/news/20081112/belly-fat-doubles-death-risk

healthy range. Joan recommends several things we can do to manage our stress:

1. Stress management—meditation, quiet time, recognizing when you are caught in your own story, consciously breathe to release tension, and let go of the fight to be right.

2. Learn your stress profile. Are you stress hardy, an optimist, or a pessimist? What is your level of manageable stress? With understanding of your stress profile you will know when you need to pay extra attention.

3. Take periodic breaks, and have fun! A key to health and happiness is allowing for some down time, and the chance to laugh. Simple things like being in nature, taking a walk, or spending time on a hobby are all rejuvenating.

4. Recognize that life is meant to be filled with pleasure and appreciation. Just believing that life is to be enjoyed puts our mind-set into a positive mode, and we can deal with challenges better than if we are perpetually pessimistic.

Since exercise has so many remarkable benefits, Joan suggested a good way of staying honest on your exercise commitment—get a small fitness-tracking device. Many of these devices are electronic now and can measure how many steps and stairs you walk in a day and some have many more sophisticated tracking and feedback features. A few to look at include: Fitbit, Striiv, MotoActv, and BodyMedia Fit Link.[16] Using these small devices and/or partnering with a friend or any of the online exercise/fitness buddy sites can help you stay motivated to keep working out. Many websites can give you feedback, data, and suggestions on your program and provide

---

[16] These are the readily available electronic physical activity monitors on the market and no recommendation or endorsement is implied.

you with additional information about how well you are doing toward your goal. The extra support can keep us on track and encourage us when we want to rationalize and convince ourselves that we have done more than we actually have.

Another key is to do stretching exercises. Stretching increases your flexibility, health, and athletic performance and decreases the chances of injury. Specifically, stretching improves flexibility, circulation, balance, and coordination; helps alleviate lower back pain; and improves cardiovascular health. Many injuries, at any age, are the result of too-tight muscles and tendons and a lack of flexibility, for example, ankle sprains, ACL ligament tears, back pain, hamstring injuries, and so on, can easily result from a lack of stretching and flexibility. With so many reasons to do stretching exercises regularly, commit to doing them two or three times a week at the minimum.[17] You will be glad you did when you look at yourself in the mirror and see that you are standing taller and looking slimmer and more confident as a result of regular stretching. Tai chi, yoga, and other gentle stretching exercises can be done by people of all ages. Try out the ones that you feel most comfortable with.

A powerful way to keep the mind active and stave off memory loss is to learn new things and experiment with different ways of doing common tasks that have become habit.[18] Many studies have documented how varying one's routine and ways of performing repetitive tasks like brushing your teeth, combing your hair, using a fork, and so on, and acquiring new skills, and using the brain (in strategizing, playing games, etc.) can help people develop new cognitive pathways in the brain.[19] People

---

[17] Mayo Clinic, "Stretching: Focus on Flexibility," www.mayoclinic.com/health/stretching/HQ01447/

[18] www.mayoclinic.com/health/memory-loss/MY00928

[19] www.helpguide.org/life/prevent_memory_loss.htm

become more alert, engaged in the world, and happier, too. The old saying, "use it or lose it" is definitely true when it comes to our minds and bodies!

DIET AND HEALTH

Food is all those substances which, submitted to the action of the stomach, can be assimilated or changed into life by digestion, and can thus repair the losses which the human body suffers through the act of living.
—*Jean Anthelme Brillat-Savarin*

Diet is a most commonly bantered about word—"I am going on a diet," (said like it is a prison sentence). "You need to diet, you're too fat," and other highly charged and usually negative words around diet are expressed frequently. Many people regard dieting as restricting, painful, and temporary. It is a hopeful fix to some problem in their lives; superficially, it is about how they look and feel about their bodies. In a deeper way, it may be about some other issues that they are ignoring or stuffing down. Food is often used as a substitute or diversion from issues that people don't want to deal with. Ever since we were very young, we are often rewarded with food as a form of approval. "Do your homework now and you'll get dessert tonight. If you do your chores I'll treat you to some yummy chocolate. To celebrate we'll have cookies, cake, and ice cream. You've been good so you deserve a reward, here's an extra slice of pie."

We are culturally imprinted with the idea that certain types of food are good for you and other kinds are good to eat— mainly those high in sugar, fat and carbohydrates—and that the two food groups are distinctly separate. The good-for-you food group is what you have to eat to get to the good-to-eat group. Combined with our evolutionary attraction for the immediate energy that sugar supplies and the satiety and sustained energy value of fat, no wonder we have problems eating healthily in today's industrial world of constantly available, large-portion-sized, high-fat, high-sugar, and high-carbohydrate foods and treats.

Jody, a clinical psychologist friend of mine, rewarded her children with green beans whenever they did something well. Her children happily accepted that payoff until they found out in high school that other kids didn't think green beans were a treat. Her story illustrates how we can frame what we choose to eat to help us stay on a healthy path.

Just realizing that food is a panacea or crutch for so many things is the first step to shifting our attitude about food. You may already have a healthy attitude about food, but it is good to understand how deeply ingrained thoughts about food are in our lives. Take the time to review how you feel about food, and try not to be judgmental. Jot notes down about what different kinds of food means to you. Look over your list and add other thoughts that come to mind; you will be amazed at the numerous ways food impacts our lives. Food is enjoyable in itself as well as for its social aspect. It is also essential for our survival, so we cannot choose to not participate in the eating process. How, what, and when we eat are big factors in how healthy we are.

One cannot think well, love well, sleep well, if one has not dined well.

—*Virginia Woolf*

Establish what is comfortable and healthy for you through observation of how your body reacts to different foods. Read, research, and consult with nutritional experts, and then follow your dietary plan. Modify it as you experience and learn more about your body's needs; you will be more attuned as you get used to paying attention. In general, as both Janet Hranicky and Joan Borysenko affirmed, the nutrients our bodies need are most available and easily assimilated the closer we eat to the actual food source. Eat fresh food, as close to nature as you can get it. The less processing, the more micronutrients in the food are retained.

Having been a nondairy vegetarian for decades with the rare bite of fish a few times a year, I am accustomed to bringing some basic food supplies with me when I travel. It helps to keep my diet comfortable for me and ensure that I am getting the nutrients that I need. Do what you need to do to ensure that you are eating the way that is optimal for your mental and physical health. Most food service places are now receptive to adjusting their menu items for specific food preferences and allergies, but in case they aren't, you can have your personal supplies to supplement their offerings.

This single chapter is insufficient to discuss all the attributes of food—from basic nourishment, to healing, to changing our moods, to creating allergies and disruption in our system—the power of food is immense. For our purposes today I will quote Joan Borysenko on what makes for a good diet. Joan says simply, "A good diet is one which provides the nutrients that makes you feel vital and energetic."[20] Behind those words is a huge body of information and research as well as emotion.

---

[20] Joan Borysenko, PhD, will be releasing her book on food and health in 2014.

Please be aware of them and act accordingly in a way that serves you and your body.[21]

> Tell me what you eat, and I will tell you what you are.
> —*Jean Anthelme Brillat-Savarin*

ANTIAGING, LONGEVITY, AND HEALTH

Dr. Michael Galitzer[22] has been practicing longevity medicine since 1986, including the areas of nutrition; lifestyle; exercise; weight management; heavy metal toxicity; intravenous, orthomolecular medicine; bioidentical hormones; and the important area of cell, tissue, and organ regeneration. He is a member of the American Academy of Anti-Aging Medicine and of all the leading-edge integrative and antiaging medical associations.[23] Dr. Galitzer has been lecturing and consulting with other doctors and medical practitioners for more than 20 years on longevity and antiaging. He has been featured in each of Suzanne Somers's books on health, antiaging, and longevity as an expert and authority on the subject.[24]

---

[21] Please check on my website, www.MarilynTam.com for healthy and delicious recipes and other food-related information.

[22] www.drgalitzer.com

[23] Michael Galitzer, MD, is also a member of the American Association of Medical Acupuncture, the American Association of Acupuncture, Bio-Energetic Medicine, and the International Oxidative Medical Association.

[24] Suzanne Somers's books include *Fast and Easy, The Sexy Years, Slim and Sexy Forever, Ageless, Breakthrough, Knockout, Sexy Forever,* and *Bombshell.*

What does he say about health and antiaging? His definition of optimal health is when the body, mind, and spirit are in flow. When our bodies are in flow there is a general feeling of ease, and all our bodily processes are functioning superbly; all toxins are quickly and efficiently eliminated from the body.

He explains that leading-edge health care is integrating the latest medical science with the ancient wisdom and knowledge from traditional health care to treat the whole person. This is the new and also ancient holistic approach to health care, where we are not regarded as individual organs and parts to be dealt with separately; our bodies are treated as an integrated system where each part's functioning impacts the whole. He cites as an example of the danger of treating only the symptoms in a case involving a skin infection that is treated with a steroid cream. The cream may clear up the skin infection but drive the root cause of the infection into the lungs where it may linger and eventually cause the individual to develop asthma. This common practice of treating symptoms instead of the root cause, leads to the body working suboptimally. Smoldering and suppressed issues lead to accelerated aging.

THE BODY'S FILTERING SYSTEMS

According to Dr. Galitzer, the biggest aging factor we are dealing with now is the increasing amount of toxins that we come into contact with daily. Instead of trying to live in a filter bubble, he advises that we can strengthen our bodies' three drainage systems—the liver, kidneys, and lymph—to eliminate the toxins. We are only as strong as our weakest part, so it is important that you and your health care practitioners listen to your body and identify what needs the most care; it may not be the most obvious symptom. Here's what he recommends that we do to keep our bodies healthy and vibrant each day by keeping our cleansing systems operating effectively:

- **Liver**: The liver is a major organ that handles over 200 bodily processes, including blood filtering, producing bile, and storing fat-soluble vitamins. This is the system that is working sluggishly in almost everyone. There are simple tests such as a heart rate variability test and a bio-impedance test that will determine if your liver is working properly. You can also get a quick check on it yourself with a simple question—after falling asleep, do you wake up between 1:00 A.M. and 3:00 A.M.? That is the liver's meridian cycle time in the body, and if there is a problem with your liver, its efforts to heal itself may wake you up.

  The liver's job is to filter the blood of toxins and eliminate them from the body, but if it is not working properly the toxins are sent back to circulate in our blood supply. This causes increasingly serious disruption in the body, which, unless corrected, will manifest as improper cell regeneration and eventually disease. Insomnia, migraines, vision problems, tendon issues, yellowish sallow skin, itchy skin, dark patchy skin, puffy eyes, feeling cold, mental fuzziness, and low libido are just some of the indications of an overloaded liver. By keeping your liver working properly you can help avoid these symptoms.

  Convinced now to help your vital organ work well? Dr. Galitzer says the first four letters in liver are "live"— that is how important your liver is. Here are some simple things you can do to help. Drink a tablespoon of lemon juice in a glass of water every morning to help maintain an alkaline balance in the body. Drink several glasses of filtered water a day. Juice and eat more organic leafy greens, beets, carrots, and all vegetables. Reduce your sugar intake, fried foods, caffeine, alcohol, and meat protein, and avoid tobacco and all rancid oils. Reduce your stress level and exercise at least several times a week.

- **Kidneys**: Your kidneys filter 200 quarts of blood daily to remove waste material from food, dying cells, ingested toxins, and extra water, which is eliminated as urine. If left in the body, the accumulation of wastes can cause problems like the collection of water in the legs and lungs, organ damage, weak bones, heart rhythm disturbances, high blood pressure, anemia, and premature death. The kidneys also secrete the hormone that stimulates the bone marrow to make red blood cells. As you can tell, your kidneys are critical to your optimal health.

    The most concerning thing about kidney health is that you may be unaware of any problem until the case is quite advanced. A doctor can gauge your kidney function with blood and urine tests. Fortunately, the good things you do for your liver are also helpful in maintaining kidney health. Drink several glasses of slightly alkaline (pH slightly greater than 7.5) filtered water daily; if you are drinking reverse osmosis water, which has had all dissolved material—good and bad—removed, add some trace minerals (obtainable from your local health food store) back into it. Eat and drink foods and teas that improve kidney function such as organic vegetables—especially broccoli and other cruciferous vegetables—parsley, organic fruits including watermelon, green tea, horsetail herbal tea, and other herbal teas. Considering spirulina and chlorophyll supplements. Avoid excess alcohol, sugar, meats and dairy, and remove mercury fillings from your teeth.

- **Lymph system**: The lymph system is our body's drainage system. It consists of a network of vessels and nodes that flow throughout the body, and serves as a major component of the body's immune system. The lymph vessels carry excess fluid collected from all over the body back into the blood circulation. Harmful substances, foreign matter, and organisms are trapped and destroyed by lymphocytes, which are specialized white blood cells. The lymphatic system aids the immune system in removing and destroying waste, debris, dead blood cells, pathogens, toxins, and cancer cells. The lymphatic system depends on our body's physical movement, because the lymph system has no pump like the heart that pushes the blood supply throughout the body.

When the lymph system is operating poorly, our immunity is down and we get sick more frequently, with higher incidences of allergies, cancer, cellulite, chronic sinusitis, inflammation, and loss of energy. It may also result in swelling in the body, especially in the arms and legs. Isn't the human body a marvel? And we have the opportunity to keep this wondrous creation working as well as it can!

Dr. Galitzer recommends stretching exercises (tai chi, yoga, etc.), jumping rope or jumping on a rebounder (mini trampoline) to keep the lymph fluid flowing smoothly and help your lymph system to function well. Avoid dairy, which congests the lymph, and excess animal protein, fats, and tobacco. Increase your intake of healthy fiber such as organic produce like lentils, beans, and split peas; vegetables and fruits like broccoli, cauliflower, lettuce, pears, apples, and oranges. Good supplements to add to the diet are ginger, garlic, cayenne pepper, and gingko biloba.

For all three of our cleansing and detoxing systems, exercise, acupressure, shiatsu, and massage are all helpful, and they also provide the loving touch that we need to maintain emotional and physical health, besides, they feel good. Ah, happiness.

ADRENAL GLANDS AND STRESS

What else can we do to stay as healthy and vital as possible? Dr. Galitzer pointed immediately to reducing stress. Stress is the biggest cause of premature aging and illness.

Our adrenal glands produce the key hormones, cortisol and dehydroepiandrosterone or DHEA for managing stress. With too much and too frequent stress, the body is no longer able to distinguish between a crisis and a minor event and will over-produce the stress hormones until the system is operating in a constant state of emergency and fatigue. Over time, both cortisol and DHEA production are reduced, and our body's hormonal balance is upset. This whole cycle begins to self perpetuate and eventually the downward spiral result in premature aging, breakdown of the body's systems, and illness. The body feels chronically tired, joints ache, fatigue ensues, and blood pressure is too low, especially when standing. Additional symptoms may include depression, insomnia, dry and dark patchy skin, acne, hair loss, decreased libido, premature menopause, night sweats, low blood sugar, and digestive symptoms. Yikes! Are you ready to help your hard-working adrenal glands?

Dr. Galitzer says repairing and strengthening your adrenal glands entails an entire program, which should be individualized, based on your particular symptoms. However, there are some basic things you can do to help. The first is to reduce stress. This is obvious and also can be challenging, since we live in a fast-paced world with multiple demands and many changes and interruptions.

The solution is to change what you can—your own reaction to the outside input. Take a deep breath right now, and then another, and now one more, rotate those hunched shoulders, move your mouth and jaws, yawn, gently move your neck and head around, take another deep breath, yawn again. Notice the difference? That took less than a couple of minutes and already there is more blood flowing through your body and the tightness in your body is slightly reduced. What if you moved your arms? And shook your legs? Bend over? Twist your torso from side to side? Get up and move around. Our bodies are eager to regain their innate flexibility and fluidity. We work so hard to make our bodies rigid; just give your body a chance and it will reward you with calmness and more inner peace.

Now for the diet and supplements that could help. Start the day with some protein for breakfast, in the form of a healthy smoothie with pea, rice, or whey protein, or raw nuts or organic eggs. Limit your consumption of caffeine, sugar, canned and bottled juices, soft drinks, alcohol, and tobacco. Be aware of what foods you may be allergic to and avoid them. Take supplemental vitamins: methyl B12, C, D3, and omega 3, because our diet does not provide adequate amounts of those needed nutrients. Get enough quality sleep to allow your body to regenerate. And one more thing that is a common affliction of life in the twenty-first century, too many working hours— reduce the number of hours you work and take some time to enjoy yourself. And remember, laughter solves a lot of ills!

THYROID AND HEALTH

Beginning in our late 30s and particularly in women, there is a tendency for the thyroid gland to function improperly. This can be a serious issue because the thyroid regulates many crucial functions in the body, including how the body metabolizes food, how much energy you have, whether you gain or lose weight, how well or poorly you sleep, how dry your skin and hair are, your body's heat regulation, your moods (hyper or depressed), and many others.

There are simple blood tests to check the health of your thyroid such as the amount of free T3, free T4, and TSH. With the results in hand, you can learn how to manage your health better. For the best results you need to seek the support of an antiaging medical practitioner who can work with you to create a program for your specific condition. If your thyroid is borderline low, there are many dietary adjustments you can make to help your body function better.

Choose to eat healthier with more organic vegetables and fruits; get supplemental iodine if indicated by eating seaweed, seafood, and iodized sea salt; eat coconut oil (slightly stimulates thyroid hormone production); add chelated trace minerals, selenium and zinc; and vitamin D from foods like raw nuts, sunflower seeds, mushrooms, beans, green vegetables, and supplements. Reduce or eliminate gluten-containing grains, sugar, unfermented soy products, and coffee. And yes, do exercise regularly.

DENTAL FILLINGS AND HEALTH

Another key to better overall health is the removal of mercury toxicity from dental fillings. This was the issue that propelled Dr. Galitzer into his longevity and anti-aging medical career 22 years ago. He tells the story of going into general practice and nutrition after 15 years in emergency medicine and being unable to help his good friend who was getting sicker and sicker. Finally, blood tests showed that his friend was severely ill with mercury poisoning. The mercury was leaking from the dental fillings in his teeth. Understanding and helping his friend get the proper dental care to remove his fillings and take the necessary steps to detox his body from the mercury poisoning inspired Dr. Galitzer to pursue his remarkable career in anti-aging medicine.[25]

He suggests that you go to a biological dentist who understands how to remove the dental fillings safely without allowing the mercury to leak into the body during the removal.

As a last point, he says that if you were to do just two things for your health—treat your liver and adrenal glands with more care and nurture as suggested in the previous pages—your health will be significantly improved. And one more thing, please get more sleep, for it is a powerful restorative and rejuvenating tool that we all have at our disposal.

> How old would you be if you didn't know how old you are?
> —*Leroy (Satchel) Paige*

REFLECTIONS

Reflect on the advice from these caring experts who have distilled their vast knowledge and experience into simple steps for you to benefit from. Isn't it wonderful to know how to achieve and maintain your optimal health and vitality? Choose what you are called to follow through on, and make the commitment to do what it takes to create more energy, fun, and happiness in your life. One step at a time and you will feel

---

[25] You can find more information, blogs, newsletters, and product information on Dr. Michael Galitzer's website, www.drgalitzer.com

better and ready to take on more to increase the zip in your life. You may feel as I do; I care more about how fully alive I am each day I live than how long I live. The energy and attention you give to the health factors in this chapter will enhance your life, vitality, and well-being each day, and, yes, you will look healthier and live longer, too.[26]

It is never too late to start. Researchers at the University of Illinois published a study that showed that people from 60 to 94 years of age with an average age of 75, developed new skills, more openness, and happiness after 16 weeks of working on brain puzzles.[27] Your brain, as well as your body, is constantly evolving and growing. As the media says, 60 is the new 40, so take good care of your mind and body, and choose to be healthy, vibrant, and happy at whatever age!

> Nobody grows old merely by living a number of years. We grow old by deserting our ideals. Years may wrinkle the skin, but to give up enthusiasm wrinkles the soul.
>
> —*Samuel Ullman*

---

[26] Check my website, www.MarilynTam.com for regular updates on health news, recipes, and tips.

[27] J. J. Jackson, P. L. Hill, B. R. Payne, E. Stine-Morrow, and B. W. Roberts, "Can an Old Dog Learn (and Want to Experience) New Tricks: Cognitive Training Increases Openness to Experience in Older Adults," *Psychology and Aging* 27, no. 2 (2012): 286–292.

9

YOUR
COMMUNITY

I don't know what your destiny will be, but one thing I know: the only ones among you who will be truly happy are those who have sought and found how to serve.

—*Albert Schweitzer*

Human beings are social animals; we survive and thrive in connection with other human beings, in community. We were born unable to care for ourselves and often at the end of our lives we need help for even the basics of existence again. So in the time in between the two ends of life, it would be natural to contribute and share our lives and our gifts with others. Your community is a source of support as well as a place for you to contribute to—both provide a basis of strength and renewal.

Who, then, is in your community? A narrow definition may be your family, friends, work associates, and your neighbors. Truthfully, our community is the entire world. Especially in today's interconnected world, there is nothing that you do that does not affect everyone else in some way. The production, consumption, and waste disposal cycle is now global, and we are all affected by everyone's daily actions.

How I choose to shop, eat, use, and dispose of my garbage has ramifications not only in my neighborhood but the world. Every time I choose a product or service I am voting with my money and my participation. Products and even some services are developed and made far away from where they are consumed. With our decisions on what we purchase, we are affecting what is being created in the world. We are in effect creating the world we want by our choices.

We influence and are influenced by our social networks. How much and how powerfully? Significantly, up to three degrees of separation, according to Nicholas A. Christakis, MD, PhD, MPH, who directs the Human Nature Lab at Harvard University and researches the social factors that affect health,

health care, and longevity.[1] Ask yourself, are the people around you the ones you want shaping nearly every aspect of your life? Does your network have enough depth and breadth? Are you making the impact you desire in the world? How do you want to expand and/or modify your connections?

MAKING COMMUNITY, MAKING MONEY

Janet Powers, the Head Diva of the wildly successful online women's networking site, formerly known as www.DivaToolbox and now www.WomensToolbox,[2] always knew she wanted to be working with and creating community. It took Janet until she was in her late 40s before she found that it was also a tremendous need for the tens of thousands of women, businesses, and publications that she is now serving. In Chapter 3, Life Purpose—Yours Janet talked about her life purpose, which is to facilitate connection. She did that in traditional ways with her work in nonprofits and as the vice president for Fidelity Investments, interfacing between technical and business teams.

She knew that it was her personal community's support that gave her the courage and resources to quit her job to explore an even more fulfilling way to follow her life purpose. Out of that understanding of community and its power she found the courage to start WomensToolbox.com. Now, four short years later, she has over 20,000 unique visitors to her site monthly,

---

[1] Nicholas A. Christakis and James H. Fowler, *Connected: The Surprising Power of Our Social Networks and How They Shape Our Lives—How Your Friends' Friends' Friends Affect Everything You Feel, Think, and Do* (New York: Little, Brown, 2009).

[2] www.WomensToolbox.com

and more page views per visitor than Oprah.com! Janet tapped into people's desire for connection, to share a joy, a sorrow, or a fear, to be heard, to get information, advice, referrals, and recommendations. Her website is the twenty-first century electronic equivalent of the traditional kitchen table meeting place, and primarily from word of mouth, it grew organically and quickly. People and businesses are benefitting from being able to connect with and serve each other through her website, workshops, and conferences. Janet is making money and building community. Yes, indeed, one person can make a difference and earn a great living doing it, too.

CREATING NEW COMMUNITIES

For others, there was no choice as to whether they should be contributing to the community; it felt so natural that to do anything else would have seemed forced.

> We are each of us angels with only one wing, and we can fly only by embracing each other.
>
> —*Luciano De Crescenzo*

Robin Casarjian is the founder and director of Lionheart Foundation,[3] which provides emotional literacy education to alter the life course of prisoners, highly at-risk youth, and teen parents. Lionheart's programs have been integrated into thousands of prisons, juvenile institutions, social service agencies, schools, and community programs throughout the United States and abroad. Robin created community, and, at the same

---

[3] www.lionheart.org

time, the good she was doing for the community came back to her multiplied.

More than 100,000 copies of Robin's book, *Houses of Healing: A Prisoner's Guide to Inner Power and Freedom,*[4] have been distributed to prisons and jails throughout the United States and abroad. How does a psychotherapist go from private practice, which to most people would be a much more comfortable choice, to devoting her life to highly at-risk populations in prisons, juvenile institutions, and group homes for young at-risk parents? In 1988, Robin was asked by a professional associate to speak at a prison about emotional healing. The prison staff anticipated that two or three prisoners would attend, but 120 men were waiting for her presentation when she arrived at the prison. Seeing the great hunger for help from the inmates and the lack of psychological support, she was drawn to help.

After four years of facilitating an emotional literacy program that she developed while volunteering in prisons and jails, Robin founded the Lionheart Foundation to make this program available to prisoners nationwide. The centerpiece of the program is her book *Houses of Healing.* Lionheart donates the majority of its resources, knowing that without this national free distribution only a tiny fraction of those who could benefit would be given the opportunity. With 1 out of every 100 adults in the United States behind bars, Robin is passionate about the fact that our welfare as a nation is bound to the healing and welfare of these youth, men, and women. More than 94 percent will be released back to their communities. She says our welfare is bound to those of others, and it is in their liberation that we are also freed.

---

[4] www.lionheart.org/order

In her clinical work she counseled many people on how to release anger and guilt, which for some was the root cause of their health issues. She found that forgiveness was the key to peace and letting go. In the late 1980s when she started doing this work, there was little mention about forgiveness aside from in religious literature. Robin worked with people to help them use forgiveness to transform their anger, hate, and frustration into energy they can use to create new choices in their lives. It was powerful, healing, and freeing for them, their family, friends, and for all the people they connected with.

Because of her pioneering work, prisoners and high-risk youth have the prevention tools and the opportunity to release their anger and guilt to cultivate greater inner power and emotional freedom. They are empowered to better manage their own lives, and raise healthy children with other options in life than landing in jail. Lionheart is currently conducting research on its teen parenting program funded by the National Institutes for Health. All this community good came from one woman who decided that giving to the community was really giving to herself.

After reading about Robin's choices, ask yourself, are you doing what you are here on earth to do?

> We make a living by what we get. We make a life by what we give.
>
> —*Winston Churchill*

VITAMIN ANGELS

Are you doing what you are here on earth to do? That was the question that arose in Howard Schiffer's mind when he thought about how he would be remembered when he died.

At that point in his life, Howard was very successful in the vitamins and supplements business, and he knew that if he died the next day, his obituary would read: "He sold a lot of products." Feeling uncomfortable with that legacy, Howard made a dramatic change in his life. In Chapter 5, Money and Other Means of Exchange, Howard shared the story of his life transformation from successful entrepreneur to global humanitarian as the founder and president of Vitamin Angels Alliance,[5] now helping over 25 million children a year.

He followed Gandhi's advice: *"If you want to find yourself, lose yourself in the service of others."* He started with his life mission, which is to do something meaningful, to make a difference.

What if you feel that you are already overloaded with managing your daily life? That you have no time, energy, or resources to share? Howard says you can still make a difference now; there is no need to wait. Your contribution, no matter how insignificant you may think it is, is useful. Do not think you are donating to a cause; join the movement. At the core of our lives is our humanity and community. We are supposed to interact with others and support each other.

Howard says that the hardest part of sharing and giving back is to go from zero to one—make a little shift, open a small window to make a change. People who don't share feel that they don't have enough love, and those who have a scarcity mentality are challenged to give. The only reason to give is out of love— share your passion and enthusiasm. Happiness comes from sharing and making a positive impact, making a connection with others—we are so much the same.

---

[5] www.VitaminAngels.org

Howard tells the story of attending a meeting in a refugee camp in Eldoret, Kenya, and coming home five days later to see his family's home burnt to the ground in a wild forest fire. The memory of the conditions of the 2,500 refugees, living in 8-by-10-foot tents with only foul, overflowing pits for latrines and with literally nothing and no place to return to, gave Howard the strength to go on. Friends, family, associates from the companies that sponsor Vitamin Angels, and even people who had only heard about Howard's work, all came to help him and his family rebuild their lives. He felt blessed that having given, he was now being given back to many times more.

People offered his family a place to live; others donated food, clothes, cash, and other items. The architect, the builder, and the contractors all gave him discounts and worked together to rebuild a wonderful haven for his family. The outpouring of love and support heartened Howard and his family and strengthened his resolve to grow Vitamin Angels while dealing with reconstructing their home and everything that was in it. As Howard recounts the story with a faraway look in his eyes, I am touched by the sincerity and depth of his commitment and gratitude. Ah, sharing with our global community, what an inspiring way to live!

> Life is a reciprocal exchange. To move forward, you have to give back.
>
> —*Oprah Winfrey*

ANOTHER KIND OF GLOBAL COMMUNITY

Mark Albion cocreated another kind of global community—a network of university students, alumni, businesses, and nonprofit organizations connecting to develop successful partnerships in profitable and rewarding corporate social responsibility (CSR), impact investing, clean technology, sustainability, and social enterprises. Following over 600 speaking visits to business schools on five continents, More Than Money Careers[6], is Mark's latest contribution to happiness and business success while fostering connection and collaboration in today's interconnected global marketplace. His background as a Harvard Business School professor, a successful entrepreneur, the co-founder of Net Impact[7] and a multiple times best-selling author on the subject of happiness and meaningful work, gave him the insight and expertise to birth this new and necessary way of matching people seeking worthwhile work and organizations looking for well-qualified workers who can make a difference.

Mark says his company helps people to "get clear, get connected, and get hired to do well by doing good." It is a win-win-win for everyone—the people seeking meaningful work, the companies and organizations that want proficient and motivated employees, and all of us who benefit from the social and environmental good that they do. Mark is thrilled that, once again, he has developed an innovative way of fulfilling his life purpose. He is able to do good, create meaningful community, and make a living.

> I slept and dreamt that life was joy. I awoke and saw that life
> was service. I acted, and behold, service was joy.
>   —*Rabindranath Tagore*

---

[6] http://morethanmoneycareers.com

[7] http://netimpact.org A nonprofit with 300 volunteer-led chapters and over 30,000 change makers worldwide using their business skills to work for good.

ONE SMALL PERSON

What if you still feel that you are only one small person? Not ready to take on a huge project like WomensToolBox, Vitamin Angels, or More Than Money Careers? Judi Weisbart[8] shares her story about scarcity and giving. The male ancestors in Judi's family have all died young, her great grandmother to her mother had to earn and manage the money to support their families. From their history of financial struggle came this philosophy, which sustained her family for generations: *When you feel that you have too little, give.*

Her grandmother said that whenever you came to the end of your resources, give and you will receive more, and her mother did the same thing. When she was down to the last $10 in her account, she would write a check to someone or some group that had even less. And if you believe that you are being cared for, you will get even more back. Does it work? Four generations of women in Judi's family can comfortably attest that it does.

Recent research by Yale and Harvard universities supports Judi's family's assertion that when you give your time, you begin to feel that you have more time.[9] The research on giving money away is yet to be done. People's sense of time affluence increases when they do something for others as compared with wasting time, spending time on oneself, or even getting some unexpected free time. In other words, when you give time away, you feel better, and actually believe that you have more.

---

[8] www.JudiWeisbart.com

[9] Cassie Mogilner, Zoe Chance, and Michael Norton, "Giving Time Gives You Time," *Journal of Psychological Science* 23, no. 10 (2012): 1233–1238.

That in itself will help a person who is stressed about time, want to give time away by helping others. This sense of self-efficacy provides more of a feeling of time affluence, which, in turn, motivates people to give more despite their demanding schedules.

> I have found that giving liberates the soul of the giver.
> —*Maya Angelou*

AN UPRISING OF WELLNESS

"An uprising of wellness" is what you'll feel when you embrace the global community, according to Barbara Marx Hubbard,[10] who is called "the voice for conscious evolution of our time" by Deepak Chopra and is the subject of Neale Donald Walsch's book, *The Mother of Invention*. Barbara is also an author, visionary, social innovator, and educator, and co-founder and chairperson of the Foundation for Conscious Evolution. She is the producer and narrator of the award-winning documentary series entitled, *Humanity Ascending: A New Way through Together*. Barbara explains that community is the greatest unmet need in today's world. When we are in community that deep unsung longing is met and we are nurtured in a way that we didn't even realize that we were hungering for.

---

[10] www.barbaramarxhubbard.com/site

Barbara Marx Hubbard, author, visionary, social innovator, educator, co-founder, and chairperson of the Foundation for Conscious Evolution. For more photos and information of all the experts in the book, please go to www.MarilynTam.com

In the twenty-first century we have been isolated in silos, top-down structures in corporations, organized religions, separate and often uncommunicative and adversarial disciplines in universities, professions, philosophies, and countries. The problem is that the challenges we are facing today are global, they do not recognize artificial human-made boundaries, and the current social and political systems are not equipped to handle the complexities. Barbara cites Ervin Lazlo's book *Chaos Point 2012*[11] as illustration

---

[11] Ervin Laszlo, *The Chaos Point: The World at the Crossroads* (Newburyport, MA: Hampton Roads, 2006).

that we are launched on a new trajectory to either break down or break through to a new mode of operation and community.

What are the new structures that can help us break through? They are at the same time very new and ancient—we have the new global electronic connections and the traditional localized communities. Localization in our neighborhoods, while we are globalizing our communications systems, fulfills a survival and spiritual need. Barbara explains that being in community and communion with each other nourishes us. The new social structures are ones where people can share and help each other.[12] Alternative currencies and new financial systems are also needed. Within the massive cities, we now have urban farms, rooftop gardens and co-ops. Human beings instinctively want to reach out to help, love, and be a source of caring and support for one and other—our survival and thriving depends on it.[13]

This is a very exciting and tumultuous time; Barbara shows that we are at a crisis point. We have the possibility of leaping into a wonderful new world community of harmony and collaboration or descending into an increasingly conflicted and competitive world where the winner is left with the spoils of mutually assured destruction. Barbara is optimistic that we will choose the happier course of building community and collaboration.

---

[12] Time Banks, local currencies, and shared gardens for people to barter for products and services are increasingly common globally, as an article on the *Wall Street Journal's* August 22, 2012, front page showed. http://online.wsj .com/article/SB10000872396390443404004577577352038273664.html
[13] An article by British National Child Development Study in *Journal of Epidemiology and Community Health*, 2012, describes a longitudinal study that shows people with more friends are happier, and the lack of friendship has as much impact on the risk of death as smoking, drinking, physical activity, or obesity. "Friends are equally important to men and women, but family matters more for men's well-being." http://jech.bmj.com

And you? How do you choose to give and share in your community? Your contribution is needed in this meaningful journey called life that we are all on together.

Today we are faced with the preeminent fact that, if civilization is to survive, we must cultivate the science of human relationships . . . the ability of all peoples, of all kinds, to live together, in the same world, at peace.
—*Franklin D. Roosevelt*

10

NEXT STEPS

I've been absolutely terrified every moment of my life—and I've never let it keep me from doing a single thing I wanted to do.

—*Georgia O'Keeffe*

Many years ago in my first tai ji (this is the proper spelling although "chi" is how it is commonly spelt, please feel free to use the more conventional spelling if you wish) class, I thought I learned all the basic moves easily and quickly; I must have talent! It seemed so simple and graceful, I was eager to go home and show my newfound artistry to my family. At home, without the music, the teacher calling out the moves as he demonstrated in front of the class, and my peers performing around me, I felt stiff, awkward, and had barely any recollection of what I thought I knew. It took many, many lessons, repeated questions, and practice before I was able to do the tai chi (please see above) forms. But all along the way I had fun improvising and doing what I could recall, and happily forged ahead with whatever style and grace I could muster, which, in retrospect, was amusingly minimal. What kept me practicing serenely as I bumbled along was what my teacher told me: if you can breathe you can do tai chi. (as above) I felt I had permission to ad lib and do the best I could at whatever stage I was at, and most of all have fun doing it.

You, too, can do the same thing, whether you are learning a new skill or doing something as broad as shifting your life's direction. If you can breathe, you can choose to make your life happier. You've now read stories and insights from many experts who have found their own paths to happiness and have counseled numerous more people on finding theirs. How has it affected your perspective on the possibilities for your own life?

Let's do a quick review of your happiness choices.

Your life purpose. With your life purpose identified and now serving as your guide, you can navigate through the rapids of life more easily. Have you determined where you want to go now? Your life purpose keeps you focused and motivated to keep moving forward.

Whenever you feel confused, frustrated or lost, stop and take a deep breath, and another one, feel your feet and your arms, shake them. Take another deep breath, move your jaw around, yawn, and stretch your arms. Roll your head gently from side to side and around. Repeat all the above. Are you feeling a bit more grounded? After a few minutes of these simple exercises, you may find that you are feeling more connected to your body, the blood is flowing through your system more and, aha, you might even feel a bit calmer.

Now, reflect on your life mission. Do you have it written down in several convenient places to remind yourself of what you are dedicated to? Read it now or mentally review your life purpose in your mind. If you need a refresher on finding your life purpose, you can do the life purpose exercise in Chapter 3, Life Purpose—Yours again. Here is the summary of the life purpose process. You can also access more information about it on my website.[1]

Short Summary of the Life Mission Process

1. Create a quiet space for a minimum of 35 minutes.

2. Prepare pen/pencil and paper and a comfortable place to sit to journal.

3. Settle your mind—practice your meditation or use the quiet-the-mind technique outlined in Chapter 3.

---

[1] www.MarilynTam.com offers free tips, articles, worksheets, audios, videos, and recipes to support you in creating a happy life. You can also upload comments and questions and get responses to them.

4. Freely jot down the thoughts that come to your mind as you ask the question: What makes me happy?

5. Write on the subject for at least 10 minutes.

6. Keep breathing and stay relaxed without judgment.

7. Ask yourself: What do I want to be remembered for?

8. Journal on the question for at least 10 minutes.

9. Close your eyes and review the whole process—listen for the answers—write down anything that you want to add to your responses above.

Read over what you wrote down as your core values and desires. How does what's bothering you now align with your mission and purpose? What choices can you make to be more in harmony with what is most important to you?

Now review the various decision factors in your life, your body, relationships, money and other means of exchange, spirit and community. Where are you most in need of support? How did the chapters on those facets of life relate to your current status? Have you made notes and taken steps to take care of yourself in those areas? Do you remember the particular characteristics you want to adjust? Or maybe you have forgotten them already? It's okay, wherever you are is where you can start now.

How do you rate your five decisions for happiness now? Do a pie chart like the one you did in Chapter 4, One Step At A Time. Draw a simple circle to represent the total amount of time and energy you have. Divide the circle into pie-shape pieces in the approximate sizes that you allocate to each aspect of your life: your body, relationships, money and other means of exchange, spiritual life and your community.

Review what you've put down. Have you made any adjustments to the way you view your allocation of energy and time now as compared to before you read about the five decisions? What thoughts do you have about your choices? Have you started to implement the changes you chose to make? It's exciting to have a fresh way of viewing your life and the decisions you make, isn't it?

Enlist your partner, spouse, family, friends, and colleagues to join you in this journey. Share the book with them. You will enjoy the support and camaraderie and your relationships will benefit from the collaborations. Please check on my website— www.MarilynTam.com—for additional audio, video, and printed tools and information to assist you on your journey. You can also use the website to upload and share your experiences with others who are also on their way to greater happiness and learn more from the experts in the book and others on tips and tools to being happy. Share your thoughts on the subject, ask questions, connect with the online community; you will find a vast pool of resources to help you on your path to more happiness. There is a rich resource list at the back of the book for you to access more support to guide you along your journey.

We are learning and growing together. As more of us make the decisions that lead to happier lives, the whole world benefits. Living in alignment with our reason for being, we are happier, healthier, and more creative and productive.

Thank you for taking the first steps to make your life even more rewarding and fulfilling. I am delighted that you chose to include me among your resources to attaining and sustaining a happy life.

Please remember that this book, all the experts who shared in it, and myself, are here to serve as guides and assistance for you as you make the decisions for increased happiness. We all occasionally forget what is most important for us, get mired in the details, and then get jolted awake to try again. It's all part of life and perfectly normal—we're human! So have courage, today is another opportunity to live your life the way you really want to. In the next section you will find a list of tools, a study guide, and other resources to provide you with a solid foundation to build upon. Happiness is indeed there for you any time you choose. Your decision to read this book is another indication you are already on your way. Please send me your comments and feedback, I am rooting for you and believe in you. Many blessings and warmest wishes.

> When you were born, you cried and the world rejoiced. Live your life so that when you die, the world cries and you rejoice.
>
> *—Cherokee saying*

SUPPORT RESOURCES

AUDIOS, BLOGS, BOOKS, COMMUNITIES, NEWSLETTERS, VIDEOS, WEBSITES, WORKSHOPS, AND MORE

LIFE MISSION

Albion, Mark. *Making a Life, Making a Living: Reclaiming Your Purpose and Passion in Business and in Life*. Business Plus, 2000.

Borysenko, Joan. *Fried: Why You Burn Out and How to Revive*. Hay House, 2012.

Canfield, Jack, and Janet Switzer. *The Success Principles: How to Get From Where You Are to Where You Want to Be*. Harper, 2011.

Davidson, Sara. *LEAP! What Will We Do with the Rest of Our Lives?* Random House, 2007.

Sara Davidson offers a free workbook on her site to help you navigate the "narrows." www.saradavidson.com/LEAP.html

Frankl, Viktor E. *Man's Search for Meaning*. Beacon Press, 2006.

http://www.thecompass.tv/ A movie and book about self-discovery and specific life lessons about belief systems, authenticity, and understanding who you really are in order to live out your destiny.

Palmer, Parker J. *Let Your Life Speak: Listening for the Voice of Vocation*. Jossey-Bass, 2000.

Selby, John, Richard Greninger, and William Gladstone. *Tapping the Source: Using the Master Key System for Abundance and Happiness*. Sterling Ethos, 2010.

Tam, Marilyn. *How to Use What You've Got to Get What You Want*. Select Books, 2010.

Marilyn Tam offers free information, blogs, worksheets, audio, and video and invites you to upload and exchange information on your happiness choices with the online community. www.MarilynTam.com

MONEY AND OTHER MEANS OF EXCHANGE

Albion, Mark. *What Is the Good Life?*
www.youtube.com/watch?v=k7JlI959slY

Albion, Mark, and Mrim Boutla.
http://morethanmoneycareers.com

Tips, online workshops, and coaching on clarity on career planning and jobs in CSR (corporate social responsibility), impact investing, clean tech, sustainability, and social enterprises.

Campbell, Chellie.

A free e-mail newsletter and fee-based workshops on money creation and management. www.chellie.com

Canfield, Jack.

Website offers a free newsletter and information about teaching, training, and coaching entrepreneurs, educators, corporate leaders, and people from all walks of life to create the life they desire. www.JackCanfield.com

Ryan, M. J.

Site offers a free blog and information about Ryan's executive coaching and consulting work and her speaking schedule. www.mj-ryan.com

www.SCORE.org

SCORE is a nonprofit association dedicated to helping small businesses get off the ground, grow, and achieve their goals through education and mentorship. SCORE's work is supported by the U.S. Small Business Administration and a network of 13,000-plus volunteers. The services are free or at very low cost.

Marilyn Tam.

Marilyn Tam has free blogs, articles, and subscription to newsletters on how to succeed in business and life on her website. www.MarilynTam.com

RELATIONSHIPS

Casarjian, Robin. *Forgiveness: A Bold Choice for a Peaceful Heart*. Bantam, 1992.
Ford, Arielle. *The Soul Mate Secret*. Collins, 2011.

Arielle Ford has a newsletter, blog and free material on finding your soulmate. http://soulmatesecret.com/blog

Ford, Arielle. *Wabi Sabi Love*. HarperOne, 2012.

Arielle Ford has information on her website for "imperfectly perfect" relationships. www.wabisabilove.com

Hendrix, Harville, and Helen Hunt. *Receiving Love*. Atria Books, 2005.

Harville Hendrix's website offers DVD-based Couplehood Programs, information on courses, and support material. www.harvillehendrix .com/aboutCASP.html.

Muller, Robert. *Most of All They Taught Me Happiness*. Amare Media, 2005.

Ryan, M. J. *The Happiness Makeover*. Crown Archetype, 2005.

Thomas, Katherine Woodward. *Calling in "The One."* Three Rivers Press, 2004.

Katherine Woodward Thomas's website has information, courses and coaching about how to clear your internal obstacles to calling in the relationship of your dreams. http://callingintheone.com

SPIRIT

Borysenko, Joan. *Fire in the Soul: A New Psychology of Spiritual Optimism*. Grand Central Publishing, 1994.

Borysenko, Joan. *Pocketful of Miracles: Prayer, Meditations, and Affirmations to Nurture Your Spirit Every Day of the Year*. Grand Central Publishing, 1994.

Borysenko, Joan. *The Ways of The Mystic: Seven Paths to God*. Hay House, 1997.

Borysenko, Joan. *Your Soul's Compass: What Is Spiritual Guidance?* Hay House, 2007.

Joan Borysenko's website has free daily affirmations, newsletters, a blog, and information on her teaching and workshop schedules. www .JoanBorysenko.com

Bourgeault, Cynthia. *The Wisdom Way of Knowing*. Jossey-Bass, 2003.

Bourgeault, Cynthia. *Centering Prayer and Inner Awakening*. Cowley Publications, 2004.

Bourgeault, Cynthia. *The Wisdom Jesus: Transforming Heart and Mind—A New Perspective on Christ and His Message*. Shambhala, 2008.

Bourgeault, Cynthia. *Mystical Hope: Trusting in the Mercy of God*. Cowley Publications, 2001.

Cynthia Bourgeault is the lead teacher of The Contemplative Society, an inclusive, nonprofit association that encourages a deepening of contemplative prayer based in the Christian Wisdom tradition while also welcoming and being supportive of other meditation traditions. www.contemplative.org

Huang, Al Chungliang. *Embrace Tiger, Return to Mountain: The Essence of Tai Ji.* Singing Dragon, 2011.

Chungliang Al Huang's website has news and information about his workshops, presentations and global community. www.LivingTao.org

Tzu, Lao. Jane English, and Gia-Fu Feng (translators). *Tao Te Ching.* Vintage, 1997.

The Daily Word.

Free online and subscription print copy of daily inspiration and practical teachings through daily prayer messages to help people of all faiths live healthy, prosperous, and meaningful lives. www.daily word.com

YOUR BODY

Borysenko, Joan, PhD. *Minding the Mind, Mending the Body*, rev. ed. Cambridge, MA: Da Capo Press, 2007.

Joan Borysenko offers many free articles and newsletters, and a community for mind, body, and spirit health and healing on her website. www.joanborysenko.com

Galitzer, Michael, MD. Free blogs, ebook, and newsletters. www.drgalitzer .com

Hay, Louise. *You Can Heal Your Life.* Hay House, 2011.

Hranicky, Janet, PhD. Janet offers consultations, audio, ebooks, and video programs for integrated mind body healing and longevity on her website. http://drhranicky.com

Tam, Marilyn. Marilyn offers free blogs, audio and videos on mental health and healthy recipes. You can upload and share your audio and video on her radio show website on FMG Network. www .MarilynTam.com

Wollman, Glenn, MD. Glenn is a medical guide helping people navigate the intricacies of health care from an integrated perspective. His website has free blogs and weekly videos on various aspects of health care. www.GlennWollman.com

YOUR COMMUNITY

http://womenstoolbox.com

An online network for women and men looking to sharpen their skills, share expertise, and expand their markets.

www.VitaminAngels.org

The website focused on Howard Schiffer's dream to provide needed nutrients for children around the world. You can sign up for free newsletters and read blogs on health and nutrition and volunteer to help and participate.

www.barbaramarxhubbard.com/site

Barbara Marx Hubbard's website offers free newsletters and community for people interested in conscious evolution.

www.livingtao.org/home

Chungliang Al Huang's community website is devoted to Chinese educational and cultural arts. There is information on programs in taiji globally and contemporary Taoist, Buddhist, and Confucian philosophy and related disciplines.

www.lionheart.org

Robin Casarjian founded Lionheart, a national nonprofit to provide emotional literacy education to significantly alter the life course of incarcerated adults, highly at-risk youth, and teen parents. You can sign up for free newsletters and to volunteer in their work.

www.couragerenewal.org

Robert J. Parker founded The Center for Courage & Renewal, a nonprofit to foster personal and professional renewal through retreats and programs that offer the time and space to reflect on life and work. Newsletters and blogs on the site.

www.ewomennetwork.com

Women's Business Network, a dynamic and diversified culture that celebrates the brilliance of women entrepreneurs, business owners, and corporate professionals.

www.SCORE.org

SCORE is a nonprofit association dedicated to helping small businesses get off the ground, grow, and achieve their goals through education and mentorship. SCORE's work is supported by the U.S. Small Business Administration and a network of 13,000+ volunteers. The services are free or at very low cost.

http://apod.nasa.gov/apod/ap120710.html

Where on Earth Is Matt. A short video created to show people throughout the world happily dancing as a community.

I think there is something, more important than believing: Action!

The world is full of dreamers, there aren't enough who will move ahead and begin to take concrete steps to actualize their vision.

—*W. Clement Stone*

SUGGESTED STUDY GUIDE QUESTIONS

1. Do you believe that happiness is a choice? Is this why you chose this book? Do you spend much time thinking about your happiness? Did the book show you ways to adjust your life to align with what will make you happy?

2. This book shares many personal stories and the lessons learned. Were you surprised at the level of honesty? Did learning about experts' struggles and triumphs change the way you feel about the possibilities for your own life?

3. Discuss the ways in which your childhood, the media, and society influence your ideas about happiness, money, health, and physical appearance, relationships, Spirit, and community as it pertains to your life.

4. Talk about one positive influence or role model in your life, either from *The Happiness Choice* or of your own choosing.

5. *The Happiness Choice* uses quotations to raise your awareness. Which quotation resonated most with you? Do you have one that is special in your own life? Is there one that you have taped to your mirror or on your computer?

6. How can you be sure that it is your inner wisdom and not another voice from outside that you are hearing? Of the many voices that echo in our minds, how do we recognize our own authentic voice?

7. Did *The Happiness Choice* affect your perspective on life? How has this book encouraged you to see things

differently? In one sentence, what would you like to leave as your personal legacy?

8. What do you think about money and other means of exchange? Has it changed since you read the book? Do you feel more able to pursue what gives you joy now?

9. How did you feel when you read, in Chapter 6, Relationships, that our current thinking and behavior is strongly influenced by the way our childhood caretakers treated us? Are you less critical in how you treat yourself now? Have you forgiven the people who have hurt you?

10. Do you have a soulmate? If not, are you prepared now to look for him/her? If you have one, are you growing closer or further apart in your relationship? Do the stories in Chapter 6, Relationships give you courage to move forward?

11. Do you have a spiritual belief? How does that help you navigate the challenges of life?

12. Do you believe that your mind affects the health of your body? How did the stories, examples, and insights from the chapter on your body affect your thinking about health and happiness?

13. Who do you regard as your community? How do they help you in attaining happiness? What changes, if any, are you going to make to your definition of community after reading this book?

14. What is your overall impression of *The Happiness Choice*? Of the five decision areas: your body, money and other means of exchange, relationships, Spirit and your community, which one impacted you the most? Why?

15. What was the one most valuable thing you learned from *The Happiness Choice* about happiness for yourself?

16. Did you come away with some specific ideas to apply to your own life after reading *The Happiness Choice*? If so, share with the group what you'd most like to accomplish.

17. Do you have something you wish to share with other readers of *The Happiness Choice*? Please upload your comments on www.MarilynTam.com.

ACKNOWLEDGMENTS

My fingers were on the keyboard, but numerous people were instrumental in writing this book. Much gratitude and acknowledgment is due to the many wonderful people who took precious time and energy out of their demanding lives to guide, support, and propel me forward.

Thank you first to you, dear reader, for your gift of time and interest—it is for you that I wrote this book. I am thrilled that you honored me with your attention. I hope you found value in what I shared from my heart and experience. May you continue to grow and thrive.

Deep thanks go out to Bill Gladstone, my literary agent and friend, who steadfastly believed that I needed to write this book and pushed me until I did.

To Joan Borysenko, dear friend, mentor, and inspiration who saw the vision I described from the beginning and gave generously of her time, vision, insights, and love to make this book a reality. Thank you wholeheartedly, dear Joan; without you there would be no book.

To all the amazing experts, teachers, and friends who contributed their wisdom and acumen to the book, my profound gratitude—truly it would be a meager book without you. Much gratitude to Mark Albion, Cynthia Bourgeault, Chellie Campbell, Jack Canfield, Robin Casarjian, Sara Davidson, Arielle Ford, Michael Galitzer, Harville Hendrix, Janet Hranicky, Chungliang Al Huang, Barbara Marx Hubbard, Janet Powers,

Mary Jane (MJ) Ryan, Howard Schiffer, and Judi Weisbart. It has been an honor and privilege to work with you. I have grown much from studying your work, and I am awed and appreciative of learning more about you and the amazing ways in which you lead, share, and inspire. Thank you.

To the great team at John Wiley & Sons—my editor, Lauren Murphy; marketing manager, Peter Knox, and his design and marketing team; Linda Indig, senior production editor, and all the good people at Wiley, thank you for making the creation of this book a joy. Your help, advice, and support were invaluable, thank you.

To Keith Carlson (www.inlineos.com), my friend, web whiz, and consultant for all things electronic, thank you. You have kept my websites and me conversant and connected in the ever-changing computer and Internet world; thank you very much.

To all my friends and family who have stood by me and encouraged me each step of the way, a deep thank you. In no particular order, I offer great gratitude to Jan, Lailan, Laurie, Alyce Faye, Yungchen, Tom, Henry, Hin Hung, Sophia, Owen, Glenn, Chantal, Sean, Leslie, Lily, Gueta, and many more unnamed ones who have so kindly and generously supported me as I made my way. Truthfully, you supply me with the power and will to keep moving forward.

To Kevin, my life is dynamically balanced and so much more fun and alive because of your love, care, and humor; thank you from my heart.

And to Spirit, I give all credit, for without Spirit I am nothing.

Sister, Aunt, and Marilyn

INDEX